Don't Divorce the Holy Spirit

by Knofel Staton

A Division of Standard Publishing
Cincinnati, Ohio

D1205981

Library of Congress Catalog No. 73-87496

Preface

The thirteen chapters of this book cover the broadest religious topic possible — the entire Bible. To develop such a subject in a limited space demands narrow selectivity. Many readers would have selected differently with good reasons and splendid results.

I have tried to select in a way that would give the reader an integrated overview of the meaning of the Bible. I have tried to show the continuity of God's history of redeeming humanity. The continuity traced in this book, however, is not based upon people, places, and dates. Many readers will have been exposed to that approach many times. It is too easy to hear about chronology and geography throughout a lifetime without seeing the continuity of meaning. It is the continuity of meaning with application for our world that I have tried to develop. A reader who has never been exposed to the chronology, personnel, and dates of the Bible will not be at a disadvantage. This book is as significant to him as to the person who has not missed Bible school for forty years.

I have tried to show briefly the history of God's kingdom in relationship to the involvement of His Spirit in the lives of people. These two — kingdom and Spirit — cannot be divorced. The questions at the end of each chapter are not designed to recap the chapter content, but rather to apply it to our present-day life.

Our Creator-God is a God of love. His love was no less demonstrated in the Old Testament than in the New. He is both Lord and servant at the same time. May this book help you study His Book with profit so that you will begin or continue to submit to His lordship with obedience and accept His service with humble gratitude. And may you do both with a real understanding of God's purpose since the creation.

The book has no less than a thousand Scriptural references* from practically every book in the Bible. It begins in Genesis and ends in Revelation. The value of this book will be greatly lessened if the reader does not research every passage. An understanding of God's Word will not come unless the Word gets into the reader. But it will not get into the reader unless he gets into it. Of primary significance is the indwelling presence of the Holy Spirit. May that Spirit be yours through a personal acceptance of Jesus as Lord and Savior either before, during, or immediately after studying this book about the greatest Book ever written.

—KNOFEL STATON

*Unless otherwise noted all direct quotations from the Bible are from *The New American Standard Bible and New Testament.* By permission of The Lockman Foundation, F. D. Lockman, President.

Contents

1

The Rule of God

Genesis 1, 2

God's Historical Revelation

When Jesus said, "Whoever wishes to become great among you shall be your servant" (Mark 10:43), He not only gave us a truth about man, but also about God. "Great is the Lord" (Psalm 48:1). Indeed He is "a great King over all the earth" (Psalm 47:2), because He is a king who not only rules, but also serves. God has been serving man from the beginning of man's existence.

The character manifested in Jesus is the eternal character of God. God did not change His character at the beginning of the New Testament era (1 John 5:20). Jesus came to explain that to us (John 1:18). In Him men saw the glory (character, presence, image) of God (Hebrews 1:3). In Him they not only saw the lordship of God, but also the loveship of God. He is both Lord (John 20:28) and love (1 John 4:16). As Lord, He lives beyond us and rules over us (transcendence). "For as the heavens are higher than the earth, so are My ways higher than your ways, and My thoughts than your thoughts" (Isaiah 55:9). As love, He lives with us and serves us (immanence).

The Bible is a history of God's loving lordship. In it we find both God's "thereness" and His "hereness." We find His "thereness" through the activities of "Lord," "God," and "Father." We find His "hereness" through the activities of the "Spirit" and "Jesus, the Messiah." While the Bible gives us a glimpse of God's transcendence, it primarily deals with His presence in our world. God, who cannot be imprisoned within a time or space system (because He created both and exists above both), nevertheless invades both time and space (history). In that invasion, He reveals himself to man. Without it, man could not know God, for man cannot thrust himself into the timeless and spaceless dimension of God. So God comes to man's dimension. This is not a myth or legend. There were witnesses. God not only created man's history, but also lives within it.

The Presence of God

God projects himself into history through His Spirit. Through His Spirit, He was present in the creation (Genesis 1:2; Psalm 8:3). Through His Spirit, He spoke through the law. ("Finger of God" in Exodus 31:18 is one way to describe the Spirit of God. See its interchangeable usage in Luke 11:20 where "finger of God" is used and Matthew 12:28 where "the Spirit of God" is used to describe the same source of power.) Through His Spirit, He controls nature (Matthew 12:28). Through His Spirit, He spoke through the prophets (2 Peter 1:20, 21). Through His Spirit, He spoke through angels (see Acts 8:26, 29 where "angel" and the "Spirit" are used interchangeably). Through His Spirit, He came in Jesus (Matthew 1:20). Through His Spirit, He ministered through Jesus (Luke 3:21, 22; 4:1; 4:14, 18; Acts 10:38). Through His Spirit, He lived in Adam (Genesis 2:7); and His Spirit provides the way sinful men can approach God (Ephesians 2:18). The renewal of His Spirit within man produces a newly created person (Titus 3:5; 2 Corinthians 5:17). Thus through His Spirit, there is unity between man and God (Ephesians 4:3; Galatians 2:20). God can dwell within men through His Spirit (1 Corinthians 6:19; Philippians 2:13), and in all Scriptures His Spirit speaks (2 Timothy 3:16; 2 Peter 3:16; Ephesians 6:18; Hebrews 4:12).

The Spirit of God is the historical presence of God. The psalmist said it well: "Where can I go from Thy Spirit? or where shall I flee from Thy presence?" (Psalm

139:7). The thought in one sentence parallels the thought in the other.

The Bible speaks often about God's presence in man's history. God did not create the world, wind it up, and then go off somewhere else to let the world wind down without Him (deism). But God is involved in this world in a community-covenant relationship (the kingdom of God). What happens when man responds either positively or negatively to that presence (Spirit) of God? What happens to man himself and what happens to the world around him? That is what the Bible is all about!

The Creation

God looked at His creation and saw that it was good (Genesis 1:25). What made it so good? The creation was a cosmic community of unity. It was a balance of harmony without competition or threats or pollution from one dimension of life to another. The environment was good for life, and life was good for the environment. All kinds of animal life could live side by side in peace (the absence of alienation, the presence of harmony). The warfare of the survival of the fittest did not exist. All of nature acted and reacted within the will of God; God's will has always been that all things be united harmoniously (Ephesians 1:9, 10).

Then God made man. Afterwards He reviewed everything He had made; but He no longer said, "It is good," but rather, "It is *very* good" (Genesis 1:31). Why was it *very* good? It was the presence of God on this earth in man. All other forms had their own kind of life and reproduced after their own kind (Genesis 1:11, 12, 21, 22, 24, 25), but man shared God's life (Genesis 1:26). Man was created to be and to live in the image of God in this universe. Man had God's own breath (Genesis 2:7) which is the same as the word for "Spirit."

The whole man is that person in whom God's Spirit lives; that is what it means to be human. Man's body is made for the Lord and the Lord for the body (1 Corinthians 6:13). When God's Spirit lives within man, there is a community (fellowship) of unity (1 Corinthians 6:17; Ephesians 4:3). Perhaps the most basic need of man today is to understand that he was made to live in a fellowship with God. He is completely happy only in that relationship. Man was not made to be independent and autonomous. He is less than human when He is alienated from the indwelling presence of God. In that state, he is referred to as only flesh, and his likeness is that of mere animals (2 Peter 2:12).

Man as God's Participating Partner

Man became God's participating partner. He participated in both God's nature (His Spirit) and also God's functions. God's Spirit equipped man to share God's activities: (1) God is a creating God, and He shared a bit of that activity with man when He said, "Be fruitful and multiply, and fill the earth" (Genesis 1:28). It is true that all of life reproduces, but not as man does. Man is to reproduce with the attitude of God — an attitude of purpose and love. Not only is man's motivation different from other forms of life, but man's offspring is also different. Not only was the first man made in the image of God, but man's offspring is in God's image (Genesis 5:1-3), so they are called "sons of God" (Genesis 6:2). It seems likely that God used human conception as His means of putting His Spirit in all humans (see Malachi 2:10, 15, 16).

(2) God is a caring God, and He shared a bit of that activity with man when He put man in the garden "to cultivate it and keep it" (Genesis 2:15). The person who has no concern about ecology has missed one of the functions given to him by God.

(3) God is a ruling God, and He shared a bit of that with man when He said, "Subdue it; and rule over . . ." (Genesis 1:28). This is not rule by oppression but one

10

of service and love as God rules. God hates oppression and has much to say against it.

Man can participate in God's activities only as he remains a partner with God in a community of unity.

A Community of Unity

Man's life began within a beautiful community of unity. He enjoyed an intimate family-type of love-fellowship with God. Adam evidently learned to talk by listening to God talk with him. He had a healthy attitude about himself because he experienced God's acceptance of him. He enjoyed a harmonious relationship with nature. He could eat anything without being poisoned (Genesis 1:29, 30). All kinds of animal life could walk before him without hurting him (Genesis 2:19).

Adam's healthy attitude about himself enabled him to accept Eve (Genesis 2:21-25). We know that one cannot accept and love another unless he accepts and loves himself. And one cannot love himself properly unless he loves God (Matthew 22:37-39).

Adam and Eve enjoyed a marvelous relationship of unity and harmony with each other. Neither exploited the other; Adam knew that he needed Eve (Genesis 2:20). Each was a complement to the other. They were living as God had made them to live.

This community of unity was the kingdom of God in Eden. The kingdom of God refers to the reign of God. Wherever we see submission to the righteous rule of God, we see the kingdom of God in action. What a cosmic community of unity it was! No sickness, no pain, no sorrow, no death. Why? The answer lies in the harmony of love made possible by a fellowship with God that is expressed by living out the presence of God on earth through humble submission.

Living out the presence of God made the kingdom-of-God life possible in the Garden of Eden, and will make it possible in the new city (Revelation 21). God wants

11

that kind of life to be a reality also in the present. His relationship with man from Genesis 3 onward works toward that reality. God's kingdom is experienced on earth when His will is done here as it is done in Heaven. Jesus taught His disciples to pray for that reality (Matthew 6:10).

Before we consider that relationship, however, let us look at some results of living out the presence of God. Then we will better understand the tragedies recorded in the Bible when God's presence is neither accepted nor lived.

Follow-up Questions

1. What is the Spirit of God?

2. Compare characteristics of life before Adam sinned with life about us today. What makes the difference in each case?

3. Distinguish humanity from other forms of life.

4. In our society today do we learn more about being independent than about living in a community of unity? Give examples. What is the reason for this?

5. What responsibilities does man have toward his offspring? Which do we stress in our society and which do we neglect? Why?

6. Discuss ways that you have experienced the effectiveness of the power of love and of hate.

2

Peace Begins and Ends

Genesis 3

The Harmony of Love

God's community began in a garden, but will be completed in a city (Revelation 21). Both environments share a common life-style — a community in unity filled with the activity of God's kind of love. It is God's kind of love that "binds everything together in perfect harmony." The result is that peace reigns (Colossians 3: 14). The word "peace" in the Bible is a descriptive word that is to be a part of all the various kinds of relationships that occur in daily living (man to God, to self, to others, and to nature). God intends that peace be the normal and proper condition of man in all his relationships. Peace is the absence of alienation and is necessary for men to be complete.

Harmony and well-being belong together. When there is disharmony among family members, the family is not well. Man needs the environment of peace and love to be well spiritually and physically. Doctors are telling us today that the most effective medicine for many illnesses is love and fellowship. An eminent surgeon recently told me that 70 percent of his patients have become ill, not because of an external virus, but because of an internal reaction to a situation of disharmony. When disharmony faces a person, he reacts with either a fight or flight syndrome which in turn sets up a physical condition that renders him more susceptible to "catching" serious biological diseases. In fact, the very word "dis-ease" pictures a "lack of harmony."

Man is not to react to disharmony with a fight. God speaks to our well-being when He says, "Never take your own revenge . . ." (Romans 12:19); "Let all be harmonious, sympathetic, brotherly, kindhearted, and humble in spirit; not returning evil for evil, or insult for insult; but giving a blessing instead; for you were called for the very purpose that you might inherit a blessing. For let him who means to love life and see good days refrain his tongue from evil and his lips from speaking guile. And let him turn away from evil and do good; let him seek peace and pursue it" (1 Peter 3:8-11).

Neither is a man to react to disharmony with flight. Flight is caused by fear, but love casts out fear (1 John 4:18; 2 Timothy 1:7). To know that God loves and accepts us is to love and accept ourselves and to live the life God has given to us (1 Corinthians 12:14-27). Harmony with self based upon a harmony with God is necessary for living in harmony with others without fight or flight.

It is not accidental that the first Commandment with a promise has to do with harmonious living, "Honor your father and your mother, that your days may be prolonged . . . " (Exodus 20:12). God makes it clear that how we live affects the health of others: "The tongue of the wise brings healing" (Proverbs 12:18); "A tranquil heart is life to the body, but passion is rottenness to the bones" (Proverbs 14:30); "A soothing tongue is a tree of life, but perversion in it crushes the spirit" (Proverbs 15:4); "A joyful heart makes a cheerful face, but when the heart is sad, the spirit is broken" (Proverbs 15:13); "A man has joy in an apt answer, and how delightful is a timely word!" (Proverbs 15:23); "A joyful heart is good medicine, but a broken spirit dries up the bones" (Proverbs 17:22); "The spirit of a man can endure his sickness, but a broken spirit who can bear?" (Proverbs 18:14).

Paul made it clear that physical sickness and death within the Corinthian church were caused by the lack of harmony and love among the members (see 1 Corinthians 11:17-23, 29, 30, 33). The healing that results from the caring of the elders may result partly from the strength of knowing that someone cares (James 5:13-15). There are deeper reasons than we have normally realized for God's instructions for His people not to murmur and backbite, not to be arrogant and quick-tempered; but to be kind, tenderhearted, and forgiving. The qualifications for elders may be as significant for the physical health of a group as for its spiritual health (1 Timothy 3). In our time we are seeing some demonstrations of the power of love to health.

Not only does man need harmony for well-being, but nature also does. The disharmony manifested among men affects nature seriously. It interrupts God's balance. Paul speaks about all of nature waiting to be set free from its "slavery to corruption" (Romans 8:18-25). Just recently experiments have shown that plant life when put in a home filled with loud discord does not thrive as do those in homes of harmony. Some plants have almost died in a home of yelling and fighting, only to survive and thrive when placed in an environment of kind talk.

The kind of life lived within the community is significant to the well-being of the community and the well-being of the individual. The community of unity gets infected when people begin to act selfishly. The horrors of disharmony then begin. It initially attacks others, but soon returns as a boomerang to hurt the initiator. The cycle of disorder that brings sorrow, pain, and death intensifies and grows. That disharmony began in the Garden of Eden.

The Harmony Is Destroyed

We do not know how long harmony existed within the first community, but we do know who broke the unity and why. Man let selfishness get the upper hand. Man tried to become like God (Genesis 3:5). Instead of continuing as God's partner, he chose to become God's

15

competitor. The kingdom of God was challenged by the kingdom of man. Life began to be lived not by the Spirit, but by strategies and schemes. Peace was lost, and the disharmony affected every relationship man enjoyed.

Why did God permit it? God's love permitted the situation to exist, although He did not will it. A community of unity is held together by love, not by law; by commonness, not by coercion. Man had been given the equipment to live out God's image in fellowship (Genesis 2:7); but it must be because he wanted to, not because he had to.

God who is love created man with the capacity and the equipment to love; however, with the ability to love is also the possibility to hate. With the ability to live for others is the possibility of living for self. It is only as man freely chooses to live for others that he really loves freely. With the ability to choose to live in fellowship with God must be the opportunity to choose *not* to; otherwise the fellowship is not based upon the decision of love. Without the freedom of love, there is no peace.

So God gave to Adam and Eve the opportunity to choose not to continue in a united fellowship with God. Partaking of the tree of the knowledge of good and evil was their way out. "But in whatever day you eat from it you shall make yourself die to a death" (Genesis 2:17; original translation from Greek Old Testament). As long as they did not partake, they were choosing to live in fellowship with God and each other.

Eventually the devil persuaded the woman to think more of herself than of God (Genesis 3:6). Her sin was the act of autonomous rebellion — independent individualism. Sin is always an act of rebellion in an attempt to gain individual autonomy (Isaiah 1:2; 43:27). It is withdrawing from cooperation. It results in separation, alienation, and disharmony.

Adam and Eve experienced "a death" when they sinned. They did not die physically or mentally, but they did die essentially. They became separated from the indwelling presence of God's own Spirit of life (Genesis 2:7; Isaiah 59:2; John 6:63). That separation is symbolized by the expulsion from the garden and the isolation from the tree of life (Genesis 3:23, 24).

Without the indwelling of the Spirit of God, man was no longer internally equipped to live God's kind of life — to mirror God's image, His glory. The fruit of the Spirit (Galatians 5:22, 23) was replaced with the works of the flesh (Galatians 5:19-21). In essence, man was no longer whole but was, in a real sense, incomplete. He was now in need of a new birth, a new creation, a regeneration, a restoration — the renewal of the Holy Spirit. A complex theory of sociology, psychology, or political science will not accomplish the completion of man (read and relate: John 3; Romans 6; Titus 3:5; 2 Corinthians 5:17; Matthew 17:11-13; Romans 8:9-11; Ephesians 4:24).

This alienation from the inner life of God affected every relationship of man. Contention replaced contentment; factions replaced fellowship; disharmony replaced peace. Instead of having an open fellowship with God, man hid from God (Genesis 3:8). Instead of an acceptance of himself, man was ashamed (Genesis 3:10). The unity with others gave way to disunity (Genesis 3:11-13). Even the peace with nature was disrupted (Genesis 3:17-19). And remember this was the will of man, not of God. Man himself had earned the wages of sin (Romans 6:23). God only announced the consequences would indeed be actualized.

But There Is Hope

As soon as peace was lost, God began to look toward the restoration of peace (Genesis 3:15). While Satan acted to destroy the works of God, a Savior is promised to come to destroy the works of Satan (1 John 3:8), and God will later promise a covenant of peace (Isaiah 54:

17

10; 57:19; Ezekiel 34:25-31; 37:26). The coming Messiah will bring peace to the nations (Isaiah 53) by taking on himself the sins of humanity that separate man from God (Isaiah 53:6; 2 Corinthians 5:21; 1 Peter 2:21-24). He will become separated *for* man, so that in His death, man will have received his condemnation (Romans 6; 8:1). Therefore, man can again receive God's Spirit of life (Romans 7:6). The good news of Jesus' death and resurrection is indeed God's gospel of peace for all men (Acts 10:36; Ephesians 2:17; 6:15). In Christ a renewed fellowship can happen (Colossians 1:19-22).

Before that takes place, the earth will be filled with the horrors of man living independently from God, and with the activities of God to direct humanity toward sensing the need for the restoration of His Spirit within man.

Follow-up Questions

1. What are some of the major problems that prevent us from living in harmony with one another today? a. In the home? b. In the church? c. In the community?

2. Why do we often fight back or flee? What are the circumstances in life that cause you to fight or flee? How does the reaction affect your relationship with others close to you?

3. In what ways do we try to act like God today?

4. Why is independent autonomy so important to us?

5. What does it mean to die "essentially"?

3

The Rule of Man

Genesis 4—12

Growth of the Kingdom of Man

Only life lived by the Spirit of God can maintain a community of unity. When humble submission to God's righteous rule gives way to arrogant demands for rights, the kingdom of God is replaced by the kingdom of man. Life by strategies and schemes will always bear the fruit of strife. This is the history of life lived apart from the inner power of God's Spirit.

The first sons of Adam and Eve continue to show the character of life lived apart from submission to God's Spirit. The Cain-Abel incident was an actual event as attested to by New Testament writers (Hebrews 11:4; 1 John 3:12; Jude 11). It is a classic example of how man had reversed God's priority of values. To be in submission means to live *under* another's *mission*. But rebellious man will not do that. God had willed that man love Him and others and dominate over things, but Cain loved things and dominated over his brother. Rather than humbly submitting to God's rule, Cain decided to advance himself by strategies and schemes.

But why? It is safe to say that all sins are rooted in either ignorance of or disbelief in God's will and promises. The significance of Abel's sacrifice over Cain's is to be found in belief and disbelief, not in the fact that one was a blood sacrifice and the other was not. God did not expect Cain to give what he did not have; he was a grain farmer, not an animal farmer (Genesis 4:2). Cain's offering is described merely as "an offering of the fruit of the ground." It was not the best; after all, if one gives away the best, he will potentially lose the premium

19

seed for a better crop next season. Abel's offering was "of the firstlings of his flock and of their fat portions." Abel gave the best he had out of trust to God (Hebrews 11:4; Numbers 18:29-32). Evidently Cain trusted his grain and his own efforts more than he trusted God for another good crop. Sin was "crouching at the door" when Cain gave his offering (Genesis 4:7).

Cain was essentially selfish. Disbelief in God's promise is often, if not always, rooted in selfishness which is expressed in some kind of self-assertion. It's the decision to live under self-mission rather than under God's. Its ugly head is seen constantly throughout the Old Testament.

The schemes of the kingdom of man continued to multiply until "every intent of the thoughts of his heart was only evil continually" (Genesis 6:5). Grieving God's Spirit had become the style of life (Genesis 6:6; see also Isaiah 63:10 and Ephesians 4:30). It was God's love that put a stop to the degenerate living.

God's "Shower of Love"

The flood was God's way not to give up all history to the ways of the devil. God will bring His promise of Genesis 3:15 to reality. He has promised that man will experience the kingdom of God, and He will carry out that plan (Isaiah 14:24, 27).

The flood purged the polluted earth by destroying all life (Genesis 7:22, 23). His grace provided the means for a fresh start. God emphasized with the four surviving families what He had emphasized with earth's first family. Man was God's partner in essence (Genesis 9:6) and was to be His partner in function (Genesis 9:1, 2). God reassured Noah that He would provide (Genesis 9:3). Noah needed to continue to believe as he had previously; however, it was not long before Noah forgot that God would provide daily. So he took more than his daily need warranted (Genesis 9:21). One of his sons dis-

20

honored his father (Genesis 9:22). The kingdom of man is rising again. Floods will never again be used to purge the earth; God's next universal purge will be His own sacrifice, so that man can be cleansed internally and receive a new heart. Now God proceeds to prepare the earth for this sacrifice.

For this preparation, there needed to be a group of people who would be willing to be used by God. The post-flood population had come from the three sons of Noah (Genesis 10:32). For a time, the entire population lived together and planned together (Genesis 11:1, 2). Of course, "togetherness" can lead to righteousness or wickedness depending upon the character of the group. The character of this group eventually became more bad than good. This happened because the Spirit of God did not rule their hearts. The group decided to assert themselves by arrogant revolution. They decided to invade heaven (Genesis 11:3, 4). Whether or not this could have been done is beside the point. The point is that they attempted to make a name for themselves and insure security by prideful self-assertion (Genesis 11:4).

It was God's love for humanity that confused their language to squelch the depth of evil (Genesis 11:6, 7). This event precipitated the scattering of the people into many places (Genesis 11:9). It was probably out of this scattering that cultural and physical differences came to be.

God Calls a Group

The event at Babel indicated that men needed a special preparation before they would accept God's salvation which was promised in Genesis 3:15. Thus God decided to call out of the vast population a group of people through whom He could communicate to everyone His characteristics, His will, and His promises. Through His relationship with this people, all people could see an object lesson of God's faithfulness to His promises, that He is love, that He is Lord, that He is an exacting God. He requires what He demands; His grace is not cheap. He is love, but not a push-over. He has mercy, but He is not wishy-washy. He is meek, but not weak. He is God, Lord of the history of humanity!

God's call to a special people began with a call to one man — Abram. His call to Abram involved both privilege — "I will bless you" — and purpose — "You shall be a blessing" (Genesis 12:2). God's call always involves these two dimensions. Failure to keep them together results in spiritual decay. An emphasis on privilege will produce pride. An emphasis on purpose only will produce doubt and insecurities.

Part of Abram's purpose was to teach his children to keep God's way (Genesis 18:19). The teaching of God's will to one generation by another was to be a perpetual purpose of Israel (Deuteronomy 6:6-9). But she later forgot that purpose (Judges 2:10).

The nation to come from Abram soon misunderstood its purpose. God has a *universal* purpose — that all nations might know of God and be blessed, but the Israelites eventually narrowed God's plan to include only them. They began to think that God loved only them. They did not comprehend the truth that God selected them because He loved all people and wanted all to know about Him through them. They were to be a kingdom of priests (Exodus 19:6) for all families, not just for themselves (Genesis 12:3). They were to love their neighbors (Leviticus 19:18), but they hated anyone who was not a Jew. They were to be a light to the nations (Isaiah 42:6), but they turned light into darkness (Isaiah 5:20) so the Gentiles never learned much about God from the Israelites. They were to have a servant's attitude, but developed a superior's attitude (Isaiah 42:19, 20). They were to be God's vineyard which He planted, provided, and cared for in order that fruit might be produced; but they did not produce (Isaiah 5:1-7). They were to

22

spread the word about the promised Messiah, but they began to teach that salvation rested in them and their traditions.

The Israelites knew that God's salvation rested in the offspring of Abraham, but they thought they only were Abraham's offspring and thus salvation rested in them. Generations later Paul made it clear that the promise of salvation to Abraham was in a single offspring (Jesus) not in offsprings (plural — individuals — Galatians 3: 15-18). All those in Jesus, not all those in Judaism, shall inherit the promises made to Abraham (Isaiah 43:9; Galatians 3:14, 26-29; Romans 2:25-29; relate to Romans 9:6-8 and Galatians 4:21-31). The ugly truth is that the descendents of Abraham failed to communicate the promised Messiah to those outside Judaism. In fact, they did not do a very good job keeping the hope alive in Judaism. We will see that many learned more from paganism than vice versa. They accepted pagan gods rather than replaced them.

We will find that there were three major barriers to the acceptance of Christianity after Jesus came to earth — the disbelief of many Jews, the lack of the preparation of the Gentiles, and the fellowship problem between Jewish Christians and Gentile Christians. All of these barriers can be traced to the narrow and superior attitude of some Jews. The universal concern of God for *all* was not kept alive. We see its suppression throughout the history of Israel. Perhaps nowhere is it better depicted than in the life of Jonah who could not stand the thought of preaching to the Assyrians. After he finally did, he wept over their acceptance of the message and God's acceptance of them. Jonah failed to see that the Assyrians who heard him did what Abraham had done — believed and then acted upon the belief.

The question is, when will Israel show a similar kind of faith? To that we shall now turn our attention. It is not a pretty history, but a petty one.

Follow-up Questions

1. Are we living under God's mission or our own? How can we evaluate which?

2. Does the church seem to depend more upon strategies than the Spirit?

3. In what ways can we "kill" a brother?

4. What does Genesis 10:32 say to our racial polarizations today?

5. In what ways do men today try to make a name for themselves by self-assertion? How about you?

6. What responsibilities did old Israel have that the church has? Are attitudes similar?

7. What contemporary expressions of plans made at Babel do we see today?

4

Faith Produces a Nation

Genesis 12—Exodus 19

God's Covenant

God called Abram to both privilege and purpose and intended that Abram father an entire nation that would participate in the privilege-purpose covenant-call. The Israelites did look upon Abram as their father (Matthew 1:1; 3:9; Luke 16:24), but how was the *nation* to participate in that call that was given to *one man?*

Since God was eternal, He would always be faithful to the covenant that was an everlasting covenant (Genesis 17:7). God's part of the covenant was, "I will be their God" (Genesis 17:8), meaning, "I will not forsake them. My love is steadfast." The individuals making up the nation, on the other hand, would die and others would be born; therefore, each generation had to renew its part of the covenant which was, "Walk before Me, and be blameless" (Genesis 17:1), and "Obey My voice" (Exodus 19:5).

The history of Israel is a history of the oscillating faithlessness of the nation to the covenant over against the steadfast faithfulness of God. The only reason God did not totally desert the Israelites was because of His trustworthiness to His Word. On many occasions God will remind them of that fact (Judges 2:1; 2 Kings 13:23; Psalm 89:34). Many leaders will note God's faithfulness as His chief characteristic (Exodus 2:23, 24; 2 Chronicles 6:14; Nehemiah 1:5; Psalm 105:8ff).

The later plight of the Israelites will be attributed to their forgetting or forsaking the covenant (Deuteronomy 29:25; 31:16; Joshua 7:11; Judges 2:20; 1 Kings 11:11;

Psalms 78:10-20; 89:39; Isaiah 24:5; Jeremiah 22:9). A strong admonition to the nation throughout the Old Testament is, "Remember His covenant forever" (1 Chronicles 16:15), which is easier said than done. The life-style of the Jews was to be so caught up in *self* that they either neglect God's covenant or disbelieve in His promise to fulfill it. They will constantly question the sufficiency of God to provide for them. We must ask ourselves how far our attitude is from theirs. How easy is it to believe Matthew 6:25ff or Romans 12:19?

One Who Believed

The promise to Abram (Genesis 12:1-3) was soon followed with threats that could nullify the promise. God used these threats to impress upon Abram His great ability to provide his needs. After all, much of humanity had forgotten the almightly God and had turned to manufactured gods. Abram came to experience the truth of 1 Peter 1:6, 7 and 2 Corinthians 12:9.

The first threat was a famine that drove Abram out of the land (Genesis 12:10) he had journeyed so long to reach (Genesis 12:4-9). What an experience — from faith to famine! Will it end there?

The strangers in Egypt provided the next threat (Genesis 12:11-20). Perhaps the famine caused Abram to question God's provisions, for he sought security from this second threat through falsehood rather than through faith. But God was greater than the circumstances.

When the third threat came, Abram trusted God and let Lot take the best ground (Genesis 13). But his faith was still not fully mature. He began to wonder about the promise that his descendants were to be great in number because as yet he had no son. He asked for reassurance (Genesis 15:2-11), but he took the situation into his own hands (Genesis 16). Through many experiences, Abram realized that nothing was impossible with God. When he was ninety-nine (Genesis 17) and Sarah was ninety, he was convinced that "what He had promised, He was able also to perform" (Romans 4:19-21). Although natural evidences were against a birth, he continued to believe that Sarah would have his child. At that age, God even changed his name to Abraham meaning "father of a multitude," and Abraham believed it. It was because of his belief in the promise of God that God considered Abraham to be righteous. Righteousness begins in belief, not in activity. Our faith must rest upon God's Word (as did Abraham's) regardless of the opposition or apparent contradictions.

After Isaac was born (Genesis 21), Abraham still believed that God was able to multiply his descendants, even if Isaac should die as a lad (Genesis 22). "The Lord will provide" (Genesis 22:14) was the faith stance of Abraham. And, of course, God did provide. It was this kind of trust that God's special people were to have. Years later, Paul said that anyone who believes as Abraham did is Abraham's offspring and a true Israelite regardless of genealogy (Romans 2:25-29; Galatians 3:6-14). A faithful person is not necessarily one who has circumcised his foreskin, but is one who has committed his heart to be God's person in word and deed.

The words, "God will provide," only scantily rested in the hearts of the Israelites. In fact, these people are later called, "Sodom and Gomorrah" (Isaiah 1:10; 3:9; Jeremiah 23:14). Failure to believe in God's good provisions will be demonstrated in man's evil practices.

A Nation Is Born

Jacob was born to Isaac, and to Jacob were born twelve sons (Genesis 29:31—35:26) who became the fathers of the twelve tribes (families) constituting the Hebrew nation. It is evident that the earth needed a group of people who would obey God and be a catalyst for others to know God, for selfishness and immorality had become rampant. Lot's decisions were selfish (Genesis 13:8-13); there were not even ten good people in Sodom (Genesis 18:32). Jacob's adult life began with a materialistic philosophy (Genesis 25:29—27:40), but Laban's materialism outstripped Jacob's (Genesis 29 — 31); Jacob got his revenge. Trust in God was being replaced by divination (Genesis 30:27) and idolatry (Genesis 31:33-35; 35:2). Personal revenge was common (Genesis 34). Sexual immorality was visible (Genesis 38), and jealousy permeated the society (Genesis 37). Again the Spirit of God had little influence as the kingdom of man grows. Jacob's name (supplanter) was changed to Israel which means "striving with God"— the apparent characteristic of the Israelites. It is seen among the twelve sons of Jacob who tried to prevail over both man and God (Genesis 32:28).

Joseph, one of the twelve sons, reaped the consequences of jealousy and strife. His brothers sold him to passing travelers, thinking to be rid of him forever (Genesis 37). But Joseph, whom they had rejected, eventually saved their lives. Joseph became a leader in Egypt (Genesis 39 — 41) and interpreted his brothers' action against him as God's action for him. God used their action of destruction as an action of preservation (Genesis 45:5). In fact, God preserved those who had attempted to destroy. Again God is faithful to His covenant.

God used Joseph's presence in Egypt to keep the Hebrews from perishing during the famine in the land of Canaan. Joseph arranged for his father's family to move to Egypt where there were provisions (Genesis 45—46:27). This group was not yet a nation, but simply a family of seventy-five members. The family eventually experienced a population explosion that threatened the Egyptian leaders (Exodus 1:7-14). Life became almost unbearable for the Hebrews. They looked to God for help, and He answered by sending a leader, Moses, through whom God would lead the Hebrews out of

Egypt (Exodus 3, 4). God answered their call for help, not because of their faithfulness but because of His faithfulness to the covenant (Exodus 2:24). There is little indication that the majority of the people were living lives of trust in God. Moses was actually reluctant to speak to them in behalf of God (Exodus 3:13, 14; 4:1-17). When Moses asked the Pharaoh to let the people go for a temporary act of worship, the Pharaoh responded by increasing their work load. The people cried, "You have made us odious in Pharaoh's sight . . ." (Exodus 5:1-21). They would not listen to Moses (Exodus 6:9). God had promised, "I will bring you to the land which I swore to give to Abraham, Isaac, and Jacob, and I will give it to you for a possession" (Exodus 6:8). But they did not believe; and through their later history, they will seldom rise above that failure to believe God's promises.

Prior to the actual exodus, God acted in ways that gave to both the Egyptians and the Hebrews many object lessons that showed that "there is no one like the Lord our God" (Exodus 8:10). In fact, He revealed His name as "Lord" for the first time (Exodus 6:3). Up to this time, the Hebrews called any superior "lord" (see example in Genesis 44:7ff). God demonstrated in the ten plagues that indeed He is master of all! (Note: The word "lord" in Exodus 6:3 is related to "I am" in Exodus 3:14. The Hebrew letters for "lord" are like the Hebrew word for "I am.")

God not only gave to the Hebrews His word of promise (Exodus 6:8), but also demonstrated that He would fulfill it by His actions of power (Exodus 7 — 12). Each of the ten plagues demonstrated God's power over a different false god worshiped by the Egyptians. His promise, "Against all the gods of Egypt I will execute judgments" (Exodus 12:12), came true. The last plague gave rise to the Jewish yearly Passover feast (Exodus 11, 12) that was to remind the Hebrews of the time that

29

death passed over them when they applied the blood of the lamb. Years later, Jesus Christ will be called the Christian's Passover (1 Corinthians 5:7), for He was slain that death might pass over us (John 5:24). The Passover with its unleavened bread (which symbolized that flight happened in haste, thus not planned by men) was to be used to teach all generations about the power and sufficiency of God (Deuteronomy 6:20-25). Forgetfulness breeds rebellion; the tragedy is that the Hebrews will act as if they have forgotten long before the first Passover feast is observed.

The Child-Nation

It was while in Egypt that the conceived nation grew into a child-nation. God said, "When Israel was a youth, I loved him, and out of Egypt I called My son" (Hosea 11:1). The crossing of the Red Sea was due to a miraculous act of God (Exodus 14). Paul called it their baptism (1 Corinthians 10:1, 2). Maturity should follow, but does it?

Immediately following the crossing of the Sea, the people sang a song of praise (Exodus 15) that included such confessions as: "The Lord is my strength" (v. 2); "Thy right hand, O Lord, is majestic in power" (v. 6); "Who is like Thee among the gods, O Lord?" (v. 11); "Thou wilt bring them and plant them in . . . the place, O Lord, which Thou hast made for Thy dwelling" (v. 17); and "The Lord shall reign forever and ever" (v. 18). It sounds like a church worship service on a Sunday morning. The problem is that Monday is just hours away; then the words sung will be tested. Are they words of meaning or just words put to music?

Their Monday came soon. They entered into a wilderness. Just three days after the miraculous crossing and the magnificent chorus, they complained about lack of water (Exodus 15:22-24). Soon they cried that it would have been better to die in Egypt with food than to have been brought into a wilderness to starve (Exodus 16:3). Indications are that they did not believe God's word or God's actions in the plagues and the crossing. They could not think beyond their own abilities. If there was no food and no apparent way to get it, they felt they would surely die.

As always, God's love answered their cry. He provided their daily food in ways they did not expect (Exodus 16). We should not be surprised, for His ways are not our ways (Isaiah 55:8). I wonder if we believe enough to pray in faith, "Give us our daily bread"? Is there really a need to pray that prayer if we have a job, or food stamps, and a well-stocked freezer or supermarket? Or if we are in college with the cafeteria bill prepaid? Is it not true that God's provisions are often not recognized as His? The "Godufactured" is often covered up by the manufactured. And if we have seen God providing for our daily needs, we soon forget. That is the story of the Israelites, for soon they cried out again, "Why, now, have you brought us up from Egypt, to kill us?" (Exodus 17:3).

Although the people murmured and complained, God reaffirmed His covenant with them at Mount Sinai: "If you will indeed obey My voice and keep My covenant [purpose], then you shall be My own possession [privilege] . . . and . . . a kingdom of priests and a holy nation" (Exodus 19:5, 6). The people responded by affirming their responsibilities: "All that the Lord has spoken we will do" (Exodus 19:8). The question is — were those words as transient as those of the song, or will they last longer? Their next action is revealing.

31

Follow-up Questions

1. List some promises or commands in the New Testament that are difficult to believe. (Begin with Matthew 6:25ff; Romans 12:19; Matthew 28:19, 20; James 2:14ff; Romans 8:28.) What practical things could be done to show we believe them?

2. How did the various threats to Abram prove that God was able? Share some circumstances in your life that have demonstrated the sufficiency of God.

3. Discuss "the Lord will provide" as a viable stance for us today. Why is it difficult or easy to believe? Do we teach it to our children?

4. Where have you seen the grace of God in action thus far in the Old Testament?

5. Why did God initiate the ten plagues? How should we interpret events in history today?

6. How should we apply Moses' advice in Deuteronomy 6:20-25?

7. Discuss words of songs we sing that our lives may not show that we believe.

5

Vascillating Nation vs. Steadfast God

Exodus 19—Judges 24

God's Governing Plan

Jacob's family had grown into a nation of six hundred thousand men in addition to women and children (Exodus 12:37). These people had not been "on their own" for generations. Much of their daily life had been ordered by the Pharaoh. Now they were free, but how would they be governed? With a human dictatorship? No! The group was to be a brotherhood, not a political conglomeration.

Moses was their first charismatic leader. Although he was one man, the government was not to be a monarchy (one-man rule) but a theocracy (God-ruled). God would select leaders, give them charisma (gift of ability) for ruling, and give commandments for the content of the rule. Moses was given charisma when God said, "I will be with you" (Exodus 3:12). Moses was given commandments for the group at Mount Sinai which is the same place where he had earlier received charisma (Mount Sinai and Mount Horeb are synonymous).

God's commands were given as external guidelines for group living. They were not given as the means for salvation or the means to gain unity with God. Torah (law) means "to point" or "to guide." The law could not make one righteous, but could only point to sin and guide the people to the righteous one — Jesus, who can make people righteous. The law was not given because the Hebrews were righteous, but quite to the contrary. It was given because they were so unrighteous that they could not recognize sin when they committed it (Romans 7:7ff). The law made it clear that they were sinners, and it outlined the boundaries of sin. It could not equip them internally to live without sin, but could only inform them externally what sin was. Only the indwelling Spirit can equip a person to live God's kind of life. But the Spirit becomes separated from man when he sins.

Paul made this function of the law clear in Galatians 3 (read the whole chapter). "It was added because of transgressions" (v. 19). It "shut up men under sin" (v. 22). It revealed that people lived within the prison of sin and needed an escape. Thus it was "our tutor to lead us to Christ" (v. 24). The word for tutor (child-leader in Greek) was a word that described the slave who had the moral disciplinary responsibility for the children of a family and accompanied the children to their teacher. The law to the Hebrews was their disciplinarian in order to lead them to Christ. The law could not save; it only condemned.

The law dealt with man's relationship to God, to himself, and to others — with every aspect of living. The Torah included not only the Ten Commandments (Exodus 20), but also the ordinances and customs required within Judaism (Exodus 21 — Deuteronomy). Later the oral interpretations of the rabbis were considered to be part of the Torah.

The Plan in Action

While God was giving some of the law to Moses as guidance for the people, those who had just said, "All the Lord has spoken we will do" (Exodus 19:8), did not even wait until Moses returned, but cried to Aaron, "Make us a god who will go before us" (Exodus 32:1). So Aaron took their gold, fashioned a golden calf, and had the audacity to declare, "This is your god, O Israel, who brought you up from the land of Egypt" (Exodus 32:4). The people built an altar to their new "lord"

34

and declared a day of festivities (Exodus 32:5). From this time on, idolatry is a continual temptation for the Hebrews.

God's anger was tempered by His *agape* (love). Out of faithfulness to His covenant, He did not give up the people (Exodus 32:11-14). Instead, He reaffirmed His promise (Exodus 33:1ff) and His power to fulfill it (Exodus 34:10ff). God ordered the building of the tabernacle as an objective evidence of His presence among them (Exodus 25 — 31, 36 — 40). The Spirit of God came upon certain people enabling them to do the craftwork necessary for the tabernacle (Exodus 31:3; 35:31). They were charismatic workers. It is interesting that from Adam to Jesus, the Holy Spirit is not described as living *in* man but comes and goes upon certain persons to enable them to do tasks for the benefit of the entire group. (After a man sins, a renewal of the indwelling Spirit is not possible apart from the coming and reception of Jesus.)

After receiving the additional ritual and ethical ordinances (Leviticus — Numbers 10:10), the nation moved from Sinai into the wilderness toward the promised land. The people continued to complain (Numbers 11:1) which caused Moses to ask God for human help (Numbers 11:14). God answered by spreading the charismatic leadership from one to seventy others. Again we find God's Spirit coming upon selected people, equipping them for particular tasks — "I will take of the Spirit who is upon you, and will put Him upon them; and they shall bear the burden of the people with you" (Numbers 11:17). The seventy men prophesied after receiving the Spirit (Numbers 11:25).

When the time came for the people to enter the promised land, God said, "Send out for yourself men so they may spy out the land of Canaan," with the promise that the land would be theirs (Numbers 13:2). But the people did not believe that promise. Again they would not look beyond their own abilities, for when the spies reported that the inhabitants of the land were strong, the cities fortified (Numbers 13:28), and that it would be impossible to capture it (Numbers 13:31ff), the people wept and complained that they would die. They even decided to choose a leader and return to Egypt (Numbers 14:1-4). They wanted to take the function of choosing leaders away from God. Only two men believed the promise of God and said, "We should by all means go up and take possession of it, for we shall surely overcome it" (Numbers 13:30; 14:6-9), but the people wanted to stone them for the suggestion (Numbers 14:10).

The faithlessness of the people cost them the promised land. None of them, except the two faithful ones (Caleb and Joshua), would enter the land. Only their descendants would enter. Taking things into their own hands was costly. It was even costly for Moses when he did not believe that he could just "tell" a rock to give water as God had said. Instead, he hit the rock twice with a rod (Numbers 20:2-11). Because he did not believe in God's sufficiency, he also was not allowed to enter the promised land (Numbers 20:12). For thirty-eight more years the people lived in the wilderness. Moses reminded them of God's laws (Deuteronomy 1 — 33) and then died (Deuteronomy 34).

God's next charismatic leader was Joshua. God transferred His Spirit from Moses to Joshua via the laying on of Moses' hands (Deuteronomy 34:9). Joshua led the people into the promised land (Joshua 1 — 5). Through various conquests, the land was allotted to the twelve tribes (Joshua 6 — 22). He died asking the people to put away idols which were still among them (Joshua 24:14-23). The people responded, "We will serve the Lord our God and we will obey His voice" (Joshua 24:24). In that declaration, they renewed the covenant their fathers had accepted at Sinai. The words sound strangely familiar (Exodus 19:8). Will the words find the works that will ratify them?

The book of Joshua ends with a beautiful assertion, "And Israel served the Lord all the days of Joshua and all the days of the elders who survived Joshua, and had known all the deeds of the Lord which He had done for Israel" (Joshua 24:31). But the book of Judges which continues the history begins on an ugly note, "And there arose another generation after them who did not know the Lord nor yet the work which He had done for Israel" (Judges 2:10). The result of not knowing is seen in the next verse: "Then the sons of Israel did evil in the sight of the Lord, and served the Baals, and they forsook the Lord . . . and followed other gods from among the gods of the people who were around them" (Judges 2:11, 12).

One cannot help but wonder what happened to cause them to forget. God had given them the tabernacle as an objective reminder of His presence, the Passover as a reminder of His love and provisions, the ark of the covenant containing Aaron's rod and manna to remind them of His presence and power, and various sacrifices as reminders of their future hope of redemption. He even had them wear tassels on their garments to help them to remember God's commandments (Numbers 15:38). Today we have the Lord's Day as a reminder of the resurrection, the Lord's Supper as a reminder of Christ's death, and baptism as an appropriation of both. In this country we do not have to drive far to see a cross. How can a people forget with all these reminders?

All the visible reminders combined cannot suffice when any of the following aspects is missing: (1) knowing who God is; (2) loving God; (3) teaching children of Him continuously; (4) keeping God's will uppermost in the mind. I suspect Israel failed to teach her children. If we leave religious training to an hour session on Sunday, we too fail to teach our children.

The Leadership of the Judges

The four-hundred-year history of Israel through the book of Judges is disappointing, but important. It is during this period of time that we observe a transition from an unsettled tribal life to the organization of a federation that will lead to a change from a government under a theocracy to one under a monarchy (really *man*archy). The teaching we gain in this period is significant. We learn that God will not honor evil regardless of whom the people are. The kingdom of God will not bow down to the kingdom of men; however, God will not give up on people who have given up on Him. He is ready to heed their cries for help, but He will not help if His help is not wanted.

The trend of the history of Israel through the period of the judges is summed up in Judges 2:11-19: (1) The people forsake God for idols; (2) they become enslaved to human conquerors; (3) they cry for help; (4) God's Spirit comes upon one person who delivers (saves) the people; (5) when that judge dies, the people forsake the Lord; and the cycle begins again. This same pattern happened many times (chapters 3, 4, 6, 8, 10, 11, 12, 13). The judges served as both military and civil magistrates. Not all the judges were men; Deborah was both a prophetess and a judge (4:4). These judges were charismatic leaders as God's Spirit came upon them to equip them (2:18; 3:10; 6:16, 34; 11:29; 14:6; 15:14).

We see in the book an early desire for a king selected by the people — a desire to move away from a theocracy (8:22; 9:6). Civil war broke out among the Israelites (20:12ff), and the tribe of Benjamin became a biracial family (21:16-23). Immorality increased as did idol worship (2:11, 13; 8:27, 33; 10:6; 18:14-20). They intermarried with pagans (3:5, 6). Priests hired themselves out to others (18:4); Levites took concubines (19:1); and some acted like the homosexuals in Sodom (19:22ff).

There is a direct relationship between doing what is evil, forgetting the Lord, serving idols, and being enslaved by enemies. It all begins by forgetting the Lord, which can happen in one generation. Immoral deeds and immoral deities follow. When the dominant characteristics of any people are evil and their God is not Jehovah, then their history as a nation is terminal.

Judges ends with a note of tragedy — "Everyone did what was right in his own eyes" (21:25). Selfish autonomy rises. The kingdom of man is more evident than the kingdom of God. But there is a word of hope, for history is not moving toward the time when the kingdom of God succumbs to the kingdom of man. Instead, it is moving toward the time when "the kingdom of the world has become the kingdom of our Lord, and of His Christ; and He will reign forever and ever" (Revelation 11:15). God will be victorious, even though He will have stiff opposition. Certainly the name "Israel" is appropriate — "striving with God," to try to prevail over Him.

God's new Israel, the church (Galatians 6:16), must be careful that she does not act like the old Israel. Let us not disregard God's way for our own will, His truth for our traditions, or His righteousness for our rights. We must be careful that it will not be said of us who make up a congregation or a church board, "Everyone did what was right in his own eyes."

Follow-up Questions

1. What is meant by "charismatic" leaders?

2. Discuss the difference between a theocracy and monarchy.

3. Discuss the purpose and limitations of God's commands.

4. Show the times that the people of Israel did not believe the promises of God. What revealed that they didn't believe?

5. How could a generation arise that did not know the Lord and His works (Judges 2:10)? How can one arise today? What practical things could be done to prevent it? Are you doing these? What are His works today? Do we talk more about what God is doing today or about what He did in the past?

6. What kind of *direct* religious teaching happens in your home? What makes this difficult?

7. Is your motivation for living, "It's what I think is right" or "It's what the Bible says is right"?

Study Aid A

Before we continue with the Biblical overview of the history of Israel and its place in God's relationship with humanity, it is important to discuss briefly the role of the remaining literature of the Old Testament. If we wish to read the Old Testament in historical sequence, we cannot read it in the order in which the books appear. For instance, 1 and 2 Kings cover the same period as 1 and 2 Chronicles but have a different emphasis. The next two books, Ezra and Nehemiah, jump over several hundred years. Nearly all the other Old Testament books should be read prior to Ezra and Nehemiah for historical continuity. Some of the prophets were speaking during the time some kings were ruling.

Perhaps the following brief discussion with the chart at the end will help the reader see the perspective. This integrative grasp of the Old Testament will help enliven the reading of the text.

The United and Divided Kingdoms

In the next chapter the Israelites ask to be ruled by a king rather than God's charismatic leaders. This will begin a long history of human kings ruling over the Israelites. First and 2 Samuel record the activities of the first two kings, Saul and David (this is also reviewed in 1 Chronicles 10 — 29). In ancient days 1 and 2 Samuel were called 1 and 2 Kings, and our 1 and 2 Kings were called 3 and 4 Kings.

After King David ruled, his son Solomon ruled (1 Kings 1 — 11 and 2 Chronicles 1 — 9). Up to this time, all twelve tribes were united in one kingdom (similar to our fifty states constituting one United States).

After Solomon died, civil war broke out, and the one united kingdom split into two kingdoms — the North (called Israel) consisting of ten tribes and the South (called Judah) consisting of two tribes (Benjamin and

41

Judah from which the Messiah will come).

The trouble precipitating the split and the actual split are recorded in 1 Kings 12. After this split, 1 and 2 Kings discuss briefly the activities of the kings of both kingdoms, while the rest of 2 Chronicles (chapters 10ff) discusses the activities of only the kings of Judah, the southern kingdom. Even though already mentioned in Kings, Chronicles emphasized their religious rather than civil activities.

Although the northern kingdom had one more king than the southern kingdom had, the southern kingdom lasted 136 years longer. The northern kingdom was captured and most of the people dispersed in 722 B.C. by the Assyrians. The ones remaining in the territory of that kingdom became known as the Samaritans, a biracial people. By New Testament times, they adopt a different temple from Judaism and look for a different kind of Messiah.

The southern kingdom was captured by the Babylonians; many of the people were sent into exile in 597 B.C.; others after the final fall in 586 B.C. They were later allowed to return home; thus their distinctiveness as a people is not lost. The Jews we encounter in the New Testament era come from these people.

The worth of the kings of both kingdoms is determined by comparing them with two former kings — David, who tried to keep God's covenant, and Jeroboam of Israel, who rebelled against God's covenant. Adherence to God's covenant resulted in a blessing, while departure from it resulted in a curse. How the various kings adhered to or forsook God's covenant is worked out in 1 Kings 12 — 2 Kings for both kingdoms and in 2 Chronicles for the southern kingdom. The sad truth is that most of the kings rejected God's covenant which resulted in the kingdoms' ultimate capture. There was not one good king recorded in the northern kingdom and only eight in the southern kingdom.

The Prophets

Prophets from Isaiah through Malachi prophesied during various stages of the two kingdoms' history. The reading of these books gives us our clearest insight into the moral life of the people as well as God's remedy. Although the situation is gloomy, a theology of hope rings out — a new day with a new covenant is coming! God's Spirit can live in all men even after they sin.

The prophets should be read in the order in which they prophesied. The chart at the end of this guide will relate the prophets to the kings and corresponding time periods. The following discussion will keep the prophets in their historical setting.

Amos spoke to the northern kingdom. At approximately the same time, Hosea began preaching in the southern kingdom, and Micah spoke to both kingdoms. No other prophet will preach to the northern kingdom before it falls. The remaining prophets preach to the southern kingdom.

From 2 Chronicles on, the Old Testament books should be read in the following order: (1) Before the southern kingdom falls: Isaiah (some place Isaiah 40ff during the exile), Nahum, Zephaniah, Jeremiah, Habakkuk. (2) During the exile: Ezekiel and Daniel. (3) After the return to Jerusalem: Ezra 1, 2; Haggai 1; Ezra 3, 4; Haggai 2; Esther; Zechariah 1:1-6; Ezra 5, 6; Zechariah 1:7 — 14:21; Nehemiah; and Malachi.

We are not sure of the exact historical setting for Obadiah, Joel, Jonah, Esther, or Ruth. We have not included the poetic literature — Job, Psalms, Proverbs, Ecclesiastes, or Song of Solomon — for they may be read apart from the historical circumstances; however, not with neglect of the circumstances. It should be noted that much of Daniel was fulfilled in the period between the Old Testament and New Testament.

The chart that follows will help clarify the sequence and interrelationships of the kings and the prophets.

Thus the reader will be better equipped to understand the significance of the Old Testament. It must be remembered that it is an inspired revelation of God just as the New Testament is.

KING-PROPHET CHART

United Kingdom

Saul (1 Samuel 9 — 31; 1 Chronicles 10)
    1020-1000
David (2 Samuel; 1 Chronicles 11 — 29)
    1000-961
Solomon (1 Kings 1 — 11; 2 Chronicles 1 — 9)
    961-922

The Kingdom Divides 922

(1 Kings 12:19, 20)

Israel (Northern)	Prophets	Judah (Southern)
Jeroboam (1 Kings 12:19 — 14:20) 922-901		Rehoboam (1 Kings 14:21-31; 2 Chronicles 10 — 12) 922-915
		Abijam (1 Kings 15:1-8; 2 Chronicles 13) 915-913
Nadab (1 Kings 15:25-31) 901-900		Asa (1 Kings 15:9-24; 2 Chronicles 14 — 16) 913-873
Baasha (1 Kings 15:33 — 16:7) 900-877		
Elah (1 Kings 16:8-14) 877-876		
Zimri (1 Kings 16:15-20) 876		
Omri (1 Kings 16:21-28) 876-869		

Israel (Northern)	Prophets	Judah (Southern)
Ahab (1 Kings 16:29-34; 18 — 22:40) 869-850	◄—Elijah	Jehoshaphat (1 Kings 22:41-50; 2 Chronicles 17 — 20) 873-849
Ahaziah (1 Kings 22:51-53) 850-849	◄—Elisha	
Jehoram (2 Kings 3:1 — 9:28) 849-842		Jehoram (2 Kings 8:16-24; 2 Chronicles 21) 849-842
		Ahaziah (2 Kings 8:25 — 9:28; 2 Chronicles 22:1-9) 842
Jehu (2 Kings 9, 10) 842-815		Athaliah (2 Kings 11:1-20; 2 Chronicles 22:10 — 23:21) 842-837
Jehoahaz (2 Kings 13:1-9) 815-801		Jehoash (2 Kings 11:21 — 12:21; 2 Chronicles 24:1-27) 837-800
Jehoash (2 Kings 13:10-13; 14:8-16) 801-786		
Jeroboam (2 Kings 14:23-29) 786-746	◄—Amos	Amaziah (2 Kings 14:1-22; 2 Chronicles 25:1-28) 800-783
Zechariah (2 Kings 15:8-12) 746-745	Hosea—►	Azariah (Uzziah) (2 Kings 15:1-7; 2 Chronicles 26:1-23) 783-742
Shallum (2 Kings 15:13-15) 745	◄—Micah Isaiah—►	
Menahem (2 Kings 15:17-22) 745-738	Isaiah—►	Jotham (2 Kings 15:32-38; 2 Chronicles 27:1-9) 742-735
Pekahiah (2 Kings 15:23-26) 738-737		
Pekah (2 Kings 15:27-31) 737-732	Micah—► Isaiah—►	Ahaz (2 Kings 16:1-20; 2 Chronicles 28:1-27) 735-715
Hoshea (2 Kings 17:1-23) 732-724		
Fall of Samaria 722		
	Isaiah—►	Hezekiah (2 Kings 18:1-20; 2 Chronicles 29 — 32) 715-687

45

Israel (Northern)	Prophets	Judah (Southern)
	Isaiah ──→	Manasseh (2 Kings 21:1-18; 2 Chronicles 29:1-20) 687-642
	Nahum ──→	Amon (2 Kings 21:19-26; 2 Chronicles 33:21-25) 642-640
	Zephaniah ──→	Josiah (2 Kings 22:1 — 23:30; 2 Chronicles 34, 35) 640-609
	Jeremiah ──→	Jehoahaz (2 Kings 23:31-34; 2 Chronicles 36:1-4) 609
	Jeremiah ──→	Jehoiakim (2 Kings 23:34 — 24:6; 2 Chronicles 36:5-8) 609-598
	Jeremiah ──→	Jehoiachin (2 Kings 24:8-17; 2 Chronicles 36:9, 10) 598-597
	Jeremiah ──→	Zedekiah (2 Kings 24:18 — 25:7; 2 Chronicles 36:11-21) 597-587
		Fall of Jerusalem 587
	Ezekiel ──→ Daniel ──→	Babylonian Exile 587-538 (Some from 597)
	Ezra, Haggai, Zephaniah, Zechariah, Nehemiah, Malachi	The return to Jerusalem and life in Jerusalem

6

The Fall of a Manarchy

Samuel was the last charismatic judge of the people of Israel (1 Samuel 1:7-28). His sons served in his activities, but not with his attitude. Rather than sharing God's justice with the community, they perverted it by doing whatever was necessary for their own financial gain (1 Samuel 8:1-3). Israel was on the verge of officially changing from a theocracy to a *man*archy, for the people asked for a king to govern them (1 Samuel 8:5).

Although in a functional sense, many had been acting as their own king because each did what was right in his own eyes (Judges 17:6; 21:25), now they are openly admitting that they would rather live under the rule of man than of God. The reasons? To be like all other nations (1 Samuel 8:5). God understood their true reason: "They have rejected Me from being king over them" (1 Samuel 8:7). And He knew that this was simply the present verbalization of their former actions (1 Samuel 8:8).

Although the kingdom of God (His sovereignty) is over all the earth and all the inhabitants, it is only the church today that acknowledges that kingship and lives with voluntary submission under it. The church must be careful that she does not look at her surrounding culture and begin to march to the same drummer as it does. Satan continually keeps this temptation before God's people.

The shift from the kingship of God to the kingdom of men is seen by a shift in the role of the Holy Spirit. Up to this time the Holy Spirit had directed the leaders of Israel. Although the Spirit is separated from a person after he sins, God put His Spirit upon certain sinful persons to equip them for special tasks. Always this was for the good of the community. The Spirit would come upon persons as a community need arose. This was a special dispensation of the Spirit for some, not the normal dispensation for all. (See Genesis 6:3; 41:38; Exodus 28:3; 31:3; 35:31; Numbers 11:17, 25, 26, 29; 14:24; 27:18 up to 1 Samuel — these are the times the Spirit is mentioned after the garden episode. However, we cannot restrict the activity of God's Spirit to just the places He is mentioned. Anytime we read such things as "the Lord was with them," "the hand, finger, wisdom, arm, etc. of God" we are reading about the activity of the historical presence of God through His Spirit.)

In 1 and 2 Samuel, God's Spirit is seen coming upon the first two kings, Saul and David (1 Samuel 10:6, 10; 11:6; 16:13, 14; 19:20, 23; 2 Samuel 23:1, 2). Except for Solomon (1 Kings 3:10-14), the Spirit does not come upon any of the other kings. Most of the other kings were not open to being led by God, and the people were not willing to be led by men who were.

It is interesting to note that as the activity of the Spirit among the kings lessens, His activity among the prophets quickens. That the people were not willing to be led by Spirit-directed men is seen by what they eventually do to God's spokesmen — "You must not prophesy to us what is right" (Isaiah 30:10; see also Amos 2:12; 7:12; Micah 2:6; Jeremiah 26). Even the priests began to silence the prophets (Jeremiah 20:1, 2). To silence the prophets was to silence the Holy Spirit. Thus years later, Stephen said, "You . . . are always resisting the Holy Spirit; you are doing just as your fathers did. Which one of the prophets did your fathers not persecute?" (Acts 7:51, 52).

The change of kingdoms did not happen immediately. God warned the people that a king would take advantage of them and become interested in self-advancement (1 Samuel 8:10-18), but the people refused to listen (1 Samuel 8:19-22). So God allowed a king (1

Samuel 8:22), but He put His Spirit upon that first one (1 Samuel 10:6; 11:6). God outlined the way a monarchy could work; it could work properly only if it functioned as a theocracy not as a *man*archy. "If you will fear the Lord and serve Him, and listen to His voice and not rebel against the command of the Lord, then both you and also the king who reigns over you will follow the Lord your God. And if you will not listen to the voice of the Lord, but rebel against the command of the Lord, then the hand of the Lord will be against you, as it was against your fathers" (1 Samuel 12:14, 15). God would not share His lordship on an equal basis with a human being.

"Only fear the Lord and serve Him in truth with all your heart; . . . if you still do wickedly, both you and your king shall be swept away" (1 Samuel 12:24, 25). The latter part of the statement characterizes the history of Israel through the time of the kings, the division of the kingdom, and the capture of both parts of the kingdom. Only God's faithfulness to His covenant allowed a remnant to continue to exist. The charismatic king Saul rebelled against the Word of God (1 Samuel 13:13). He feared the people more than God and gave in to their wishes (1 Samuel 15:24-26). He became a bitter man who could not stand the threat of the popularity of David. To hear the people sing, "Saul has slain his thousands, and David his ten thousands" (1 Samuel 18:7) aroused jealousy (1 Samuel 18:8). Jealousy tends to widen alienation (if not create it) rather than foster fellowship. And that's what happened between Saul and David (1 Samuel 19 — 31).

At the death of Saul, David became the second charismatic king of God (2 Samuel 23:2; Acts 1:16). The alienation between Saul and David saw an early division within the united kingdom (2 Samuel 3); however, a formal split will not occur until after David's son, Solomon, rules.

49

David expanded the kingdom geographically and politically. The kingdom of Israel (not the kingdom of God) became a world power. David was a person who usually trusted God's sufficiency (1 Samuel 17:37, 45-47; 25:32-35; 2 Samuel 22). He wrote most of the psalms. As great as he was, he was still a human being who sinned in adultery and murder (2 Samuel 11:1 — 12:6). He was able to admit his wrong, repent, and take whatever consequences were deemed necessary for punishment (2 Samuel 12:7-15). Also see Psalm 51, his song of repentance.

There will be no other king like David. His advice to his son revealed his philosophy of kingship: "Be strong, therefore, and show yourself a man. And keep the charge of the Lord your God, to walk in His ways, to keep His statutes, His commandments, His ordinances, and His testimonies, according to what is written in the law of Moses, that you may succeed in all that you do and wherever you turn" (1 Kings 2:2, 3); and "My son Solomon, know the God of your father, and serve Him with a whole heart and a willing mind" (1 Chronicles 28:9).

While David was the best king, Solomon was the richest. He expanded the wealth of the kingdom to a place never before nor ever after attained. His riches were a result of wisdom given to him from God (1 Kings 3:7-14; 10:23-25). He uttered three thousand proverbs, one thousand five songs, and spoke fluently in many areas such as botany and zoology (1 Kings 4:29-34). He was a master merchant and builder. He built a palace, halls (1 Kings 7:1ff), stables (1 Kings 4:26; 10:28), seaports, fleets (1 Kings 9:26; 10:22), cities (1 Kings 9:15-19), the temple (1 Kings 6, 7). He was a professional organizer (1 Kings 4:1-19). The wealth of the kingdom was so dominant that silver became as common as stone. However, his enterprising endeavors were not all well accepted, for he recruited forced labor from among his own people (1 Kings 5:13-18; 12:4), made commercial alliances with pagans (1 Kings 5:1-12), gave some of the promised land away (1 Kings 9:10-14), and made political alliances with pagan countries by marrying their kings' daughters (1 Kings 3:1).

Lust for women was one of Solomon's major weaknesses. He had three hundred concubines plus seven hundred wives (1 Kings 11:3). He tried to please them by building altars to their gods and thus was involved with idolatry (1 Kings 11:4-8). Instead of continually using God's charisma of wisdom, be began to rule via complex organization and political alliances. In a real sense, he confined God into the Holy of Holies within the temple. The height of arrogance is seen when he boasts, "I have surely built Thee a lofty house, a place for Thy dwelling" (1 Kings 8:13). God chose mobility in the tabernacle, but Solomon chose stability in the temple. Although Solomon clearly admitted that God could not be boxed in (1 Kings 8:27; 2 Chronicles 6:18), others later will restrict God to it, so that God will say, "Heaven is My throne, and earth is My footstool. Where then is a house you could build for Me?" (Isaiah 66:1). God had built a house for himself in the hearts of men (Genesis 2:7) from which He does not want to be replaced. When God said that a son of David would build a house for God (1 Chronicles 17:11, 12), He was ultimately referring to Jesus who would make possible a new temple after the resurrection. His temple will be the temple of a human body (John 2:19-21; 1 Corinthians 6:19).

With Solomon, the kingdom of God had been completely transferred to the kingdom of men; and from his time until Jesus, the kingship of God will hardly be seen. Religion became a state-supported phenomenon. Politicians were heard over the prophets (1 Kings 2:26, 27) and kings over priests (1 Kings 1:7, 25). The kings moved from charisma to competition as potential kings killed ruling kings for the throne. The government over the people of God moved from the deity to the dynasty, from theocracy to *man*archy, from a brotherhood to a dictatorship, from the Holy Spirit to human schemes, from the providence of God to the proficiency of men, and from charisma to professionalism.

After Solomon's death, the kingdom split (1 Kings 12ff). We should not be surprised, for there can never be lasting unity without the presence of God's Spirit and voluntary submission to Him (Ephesians 4:3). Only eight out of the forty kings were considered good, and most of these eight permitted idol worship to continue (Asa, 1 Kings 15:11ff); Jehoshaphat, 1 Kings 22:42ff; 2 Chronicles 20:31-33; Joash, 2 Kings 12:2ff; Amaziah, 2 Kings 14:3, 4; 2 Chronicles 25:2ff, 14ff; Azariah (Uzziah), 2 Kings 15:3, 4; Jotham, 2 Kings 15:32-35; Hezekiah, 2 Kings 18:3-6; Josiah, 2 Kings 22; 2 Chronicles 34).

What kind of life emerged from the kingdom of man? Let us first look at some of the general descriptions of the people and at some of their specific attitudes and activities. All of the Scriptures should be read and discussed.

General Descriptions

Although the following panoramic descriptions were uttered about the southern kingdom, they aptly apply to the northern kingdom as well. The people were adulterous (Jeremiah 31); skilled in doing evil, but unskilled in doing good (Jeremiah 4:22); they knew no boundaries in deeds of wickedness (Jeremiah 5:8; 9:3-6). They were utterly faithless to the Lord (Jeremiah 5:11). They were insensitive to sin as seen by the fact that they had forgotten how to blush (Jeremiah 6:15), so they were called "sons who act corruptly" (Isaiah 1:4). The leaders were called "rulers of Sodom" and the people were called "people of Gomorrah" (Isaiah 1:10). They were God's foes instead of His friends (Isaiah 1:24), for both their speech and actions were against the Lord (Isaiah 3:8). The intra-family relationship was reversed as children became oppressors and as women ruled over men (Isaiah 3:12). Everyone was called godless (Isaiah 9:17); they were circumcised, but yet uncircumcised (Jeremiah 9:25). No one called on God (Isaiah 64:7) and they loved the rebel life (Jeremiah 14:10).

How did the special people get that way? The answer is simple — they had changed their god (Jeremiah 2:11, 28). But what processes led to a willingness to change to another god? The process is still alive today regretfully. They allowed truth to perish (Jeremiah 7:28). The first step in doing that is not to speak the truths about God within the family. Thus God was slowly forgotten (Jeremiah 2:32). Trust in God for progress and security was slowly transferred to trust in lies (Isaiah 28:15) and oppression (Isaiah 30:12). The end of that process is seen in their rejecting the law and despising God (Isaiah 5:24). No wonder they no longer believed His promises and were full of diviners and soothsayers (Isaiah 2:6). The practical life within the special group of people became miserable.

Attitudes and Activities

Since truth was hated (Amos 5:10; Isaiah 59:15; Jeremiah 6:10), God's spokesmen were silenced (Amos 2:12; 7:12, 13; Micah 2:6; Isaiah 30:10, 11; Jeremiah 20:1, 2; 26), and lying speechmakers were popularly accepted (Hosea 4:4ff; Micah 3:5; Zephaniah 3:1-4; Jeremiah 2:8; 5:13; 6:13ff; 14:13ff; 27:9ff; 29:8ff; Ezekiel 34:1ff). Jeremiah summed up the tragedy: "An appalling and horrible thing has happened in the land; the prophets prophesy falsely, and the priests rule on their own authority; and My people love it so!" (Jeremiah 5:30, 31). Even scribes changed the Word to read a lie (Jeremiah 8:8). Both prophet and priest spoke for

53

money as their trade, but without knowledge (Jeremiah 14:18). The priests were drunkards (Isaiah 28:7). It is quite clear that the common people were misled by their leaders (Isaiah 3:12; 9:16; Zephaniah 3:3; Jeremiah 5:5; 10:21; 23:1ff).

Since the word of God was absent, immorality became the order of the day (Hosea 4:2). Values were reversed (Isaiah 5:20). There was a zealous concern for entertainment (Amos 6:4-7; Isaiah 5:11, 12, 22). Justice was perverted (Amos 6:12) as taking bribes was the motivation for making decisions of "justice" (Amos 5:12; Micah 3:11; 7:3; Isaiah 1:23; 5:23). Sexual looseness was common (Jeremiah 5:8; Amos 2:7). Evil was returned for good received (Jeremiah 18:20). People cheated and suppressed one another. No man spared his brother (Hosea 12:7ff; Micah 2:2; 6:11, 12; Jeremiah 22:13ff).

Without trust in the sufficiency of God, the people began to trust in themselves; autonomy arose (Jeremiah 8:6; 9:14; 11:8; 18:12). "We are going to follow our own plans" (Jeremiah 18:12) became the way of the kingdom of man. They thought they were self-sufficient; but instead of turning to God, they looked to other sources for counsel (Hosea 4:12). They sought security in political alliances (Hosea 5:13; 8:9; 12:1; Isaiah 30:1ff; 36:4ff) and safety in military might (Hosea 10:13; Isaiah 22:8ff; 30:15; 31:1ff). They took protection in lies, "We have made falsehood our refuge, and we have concealed ourselves with deception" (Isaiah 28:15). The lying was coupled with practicing a pseudo-intellectualism (Isaiah 5:21).

Their selfish hearts created a dominating concern for the personal and private accumulation of material wealth (Amos 8:4ff; Hosea 7:14; Micah 2:2; Jeremiah 6:13; 22:17; Isaiah 5:8). That goal justified any means. Care for the poor was sidetracked (Amos 2:7; 4:1ff; 5:11ff; Isaiah 1:23; Jeremiah 2:34; 5:28). Perhaps the

54

greatest tragedy of all is seen in the fact that they would not admit they were faltering (Jeremiah 2:23, 25; 8:8); so they would not accept correction (Jeremiah 2:30; 5:3; 7:28; Zephaniah 3:2). In a real sense, they tried to change roles with God.

While all of this was happening, they never forsook "worship." However, their worship was just mechanical. It was made of words only (Hosea 10:4). It was a religious formalism without social responsibility, and God hated that kind of worship (Amos 5:18ff; Jeremiah 7:8ff; Hosea 6:6; 8:13; Isaiah 1:11ff). When will God's people learn that duty is not taken care of by just attending the regular services? The following words were not spoken to outsiders, but they were spoken to those "people of God" who regularly attended the services but did not manifest God's characteristics within society: "Come now, and let us reason together, says the Lord, though your sins are as scarlet, they will be as white as snow; though they are red like crimson, they will become like wool" (Isaiah 1:18, see the wider context from 1:1-17). Although Israel had her worship on the Sabbath, she had her idols for the other days. The idols were mentioned more than any other single thing (Jeremiah 5:19; 7:18; 18:15; 19:4ff; Amos 7:9; Hosea 3:1; 4:13; 8:4, 11, 14; 9:10; 10:1ff; 11:2; 13:1ff; Micah 1:6ff).

This is a grim picture. It is easy to find parallels between the living of that group of people and our nation.

A nation is not God's "new Israel" empowered by God's Holy Spirit to live God's image on earth in a covenant-relationship with Him. A kingdom of man does not equal the kingdom of God. Only redeemed people make up the membership of God's "new Israel" — the church. We should not expect the unregenerate population of any nation to live any other way than as described in the foregoing pages. We cannot expect a nation to change unless it is converted. But we can expect the church to be different. It is time that we quit finding those outside the church to fit the labels that were described. We who are Christians need to look at ourselves and ask, "Do any of these descriptions of old Israel fit me? If so, I need to repent!"

Follow-up Questions

1. In what way do we silence preachers of God's Word today as the Israelites did the prophets?

2. What should be the role of Christians in a government? (a) as citizens? (b) as officials?

3. Does the increased wealth of a nation necessarily imply God's blessing? Relate to Solomon's kingdom.

4. How did Solomon turn Judaism into a state-supported religion? What are the dangers of a state-supported religion?

5. Discuss whether or not these attitudes and activities of Israel are evident among Christians today: forgetting to blush; belittling family living; allowing truth to perish; a change from trusting God to schemes, power, and military; unconcern for the poor; mechanical worship.

7

From Despair to Hope

Repent or Perish

The prophets were concerned about the condition of God's people. They spoke with both reality, revealing the pessimistic state of affairs, and with hope, promising that defeat was not necessary. However, the only way to detour destruction would be by a repentance (Isaiah 1:16; Jeremiah 4:1, 2; 7:3; Hosea 6:1; 14:1). Repentance did not mean a mere sorrow of being found in the wrong, but rather a reversal of attitudes and activities. It meant to "amend your ways and your doings," to execute justice, to quit oppressing people, and to stop worshiping other gods. If they would do those things, God promised, "I will let you dwell in this place" (Jeremiah 7:5-7). They must not simply cease to do evil but also seek to do good (Amos 5:14; Micah 6:8; Isaiah 1:17; Zephaniah 2:3). They must actively seek the Lord (Amos 5:6; Hosea 10:12), consult Him (Isaiah 8:19), and walk in His light (Isaiah 2:5; Jeremiah 6:16). In order to perform these actions, they must acknowledge their guilt (Jeremiah 3:13), and quit trying to be like other nations (Jeremiah 10:2ff).

The restoration to God's way must begin with the leaders (Isaiah 1:26ff; Jeremiah 3:15). The prophets warned that both kingdoms would fall without a repentance by the priests, prophets, and the people.

The Fall

After being warned by the prophets (God's spokesmen), the northern kingdom (Israel) fell to the Assyrians in 722 B.C. (2 Kings 17). According to Sargon, 27,290 of the citizens were deported to upper Mesopotamia and Media. The king of Assyria brought foreigners to occupy the land and intermarry with the remaining inhabitants (2 Kings 17:24). The Israelites adopted their gods and customs. Thus their identity of a separate people was lost (2 Kings 17:29ff).

The southern kingdom (Judah) finally fell to Babylon in 586 B.C. (2 Kings 24, 25). However, years prior to the final fall, several were deported (2 Kings 24:14ff; Jeremiah 52:28ff). The final blow was devastating — Jerusalem was burned, leaders were executed, and more people were deported (2 Kings 25). The Babylonian exile began.

Significance of the Babylonian Exile

A study of the exile is very important to understand the Judaism of the New Testament era, for it was during this period that many features of first-century Judaism were born. Space will permit little more than a mention of these features.

(1) The scattering of Jewish population heightened during this period. Jews not only went to Babylon but also to other places. This began the worldwide scattering that is apparent in Acts 2:8-10. This scattering eventually created a rift within Judaism. Some of them became liberal, being hellenized (adapting features of Greek culture). Later orthodox Jews did not relate well to them; however, all of Judaism had adopted some Hellenistic practices by the New Testament period. The population of Jews in Egypt eventually gave rise to a Greek translation of the Old Testament (Septuagint).

(2) The synagogue was born. This arose in the absence of the temple.

(3) The use of rabbis began.

(4) The importance of the law was revived. The exile was an object lesson that the prophets had been correct, so the people were engaged in a spiritual revival.

(5) Universalism was emphasized more. Seeing pagans with their progress caused many Jews to believe

that God not only loved them but others as well.

(6) Along with universalism, Jewish racial purity was reemphasized. If Jews were to do God's mission to all people, they must be the people He intended them to be.

Rebuilding Jerusalem

The lessons learned by the people through the exile were good for them. By the time the Persians took the world power from the Babylonians, many Jews were ready to build a spiritual foundation back home. They returned to Jerusalem to do so under the release of Cyrus in 538 B.C. (2 Chronicles 36:22, 23). Many did not return because life in Babylon was good for them. They were allowed to own real estate, farm, engage in business (Jeremiah 29:5-7), and live in various communities (Ezra 2:59). Some became leading citizens (Ezra 8:16, 17). Ezekiel was overwhelmed by their good life (3:15).

The returnees had a rough life. The city was in ruins. The inhabitants had not experienced a spiritual revival and had gone further into paganism. They felt the returnees were intruders (Ezekiel 33:24). Physical danger was a reality (Zechariah 8:10). On top of it all, the early crops failed. Little work was done on the temple. A second group of returnees arrived in 522 to find that only the foundation to the temple had been rebuilt (Haggai 1:3ff; 2:15ff).

During this time, the early returnees had lost the results of their spiritual revival. They had fallen back into the kind of life they lived prior to the fall of the kingdom. They intermarried, oppressed those poorer than they, and did business on the Sabbath.

Progress in rebuilding depended upon a spiritual motivation expressed in a kind of national unity. It came with Nehemiah and Ezra. Ezra emphasized the law, and Nehemiah dictated decrees that demanded the law be followed. That teaching unified the people so that they returned to their mission; the temple was finished in 515 B.C. (For some significant directives of Nehemiah see Nehemiah 5, 13.)

The revival was short-lived, however; selfishness arose again. The priests became corrupt (Malachi 1:6 — 2:9). The people were little better (Malachi 2:10; 3: 5ff); values were again reversed (Malachi 2:17). What was needed? Nothing short of a heavenly king — God — ruling over the hearts of man. Only then will the "day of the Lord come." To this the prophets pointed as they spoke about the realities of old Israel.

The Prophets of Hope

Although the prophets spoke of the coming doom of the kingdom, they spoke words of hope. Isaiah spoke about the fall of Babylon and the freedom following the exile (41:25; 42:22; 43:14, 28; 44:26ff; 45:1ff; 47:1ff; 48:14, 20). But their primary hope lay beyond the mere physical restoration of Jerusalem to the restoration of God's kingdom on earth. Thus they spoke about a new day to come. That period was called the "latter or last days," the "day of the Lord," and the "kingdom of God."

These are the characteristics of the new kingdom: (1) *Righteousness* will prevail (Hosea 2:19; Isaiah 32: 16ff; 33:15) because the law of God will be known (Hosea 6:3), and hearts will be committed (Jeremiah 4:4). (2) *All peoples* will be included (not just Jews, Micah 4:1ff; 5:3; Isaiah 2:2ff; 11:10ff; 26:2; 33:13; Jeremiah 3:17 — "far off" and "near" refer to Gentile and Jew — see Ephesians 2:13; Isaiah 57:19). (3) *Forgiveness* will be extended (Isaiah 33:24; Jeremiah 31:34). (4) The *Messiah* will come (Micah 5:2; Isaiah 4:2; 7:14; 9:2ff; 11:1ff; 32:1; 42:1ff; 49:1ff; 52:13ff; 53:1ff; 61:1ff; 65:1; Jeremiah 23:5ff; 33:15ff; Zechariah 3:8; 6:12, 13). (5) The *Holy Spirit* will again live within the people (Jeremiah 31:31ff; Ezekiel 11:19; 36:26, 27; 37:14; 39:29; Joel 2:28ff).

All of these characteristics are related. The Messiah shall take man's sin as His own and thus experience separation from God for man (Isaiah 53; 2 Corinthians 5:21). That act will provide the reality for forgiveness and prepare the sinful heart (by cleansing it) to be again the dwelling place for the Holy Spirit. God's Spirit will again live in men producing the fruit of the spirit — righteousness (Isaiah 32:15ff). This is for all people, those far off (Gentiles) and those near (Jews, Acts 2:39). Those who obey will all be called priests (Isaiah 61:6; see 1 Peter 2:9). The temple of mortar will be replaced by the temple of men — a binding of many bodies. Whoever receives God's Spirit within him will not only be united to God, but also to all others who possess God's Spirit. A *koinonia* (fellowship of commonness — oneness) will result. All those so united will constitute God's "new Israel" — the church (Galatians 6:10) — and God's "new temple" (1 Corinthians 3:16; Ephesians 2:21ff).

The church will be God's "new way" (Isaiah 43:19). People will be redeemed for service (Isaiah 43:21, relate to Ephesians 2:10; 1 Peter 1:22) by a Savior (Isaiah 43:1; 45:22; 46:12, 13). God's own anointed King will come (Isaiah 9:6, 7; 44:6ff) to live on the earth and later inside men (John 17:26). Indeed God will make a way in the wilderness that Israel had planted. Instead of circumcision, Christ will be given as a covenant to the people (Isaiah 42:6). He is God's new covenant (testament). It is God's restoration movement (Isaiah 49:6) to restore in the midst of a decayed creation, a new creation (2 Corinthians 5:17) by a renewal of the Holy Spirit within men as an act of spiritual regeneration (John 3; Titus 3:5).

The prophets also spoke a word of hope that stretches beyond the restoration of God's kingdom on this earth. Isaiah spoke also about a new Heaven and a new earth (Isaiah 65:17; 66:22ff). So the prophets spoke about

God's grace for the Babylonian era, the Christian era, and the timeless era following the second coming of the Christ.

The Jews looked for a Messiah but for a different one than God promised. Why? The next section will help us understand and appreciate why.

The Intertestamental Period

By the time Jesus came, the Messianic expectation of the Jews had become an expectation for a political king. They were looking for a human king to again rule the kingdom of men rather than for a visit of God in flesh. There are two reasons for the political wish: (1) their misunderstanding of Scripture; they misapplied such passages as Isaiah 9:6ff and did not apply such passages as Isaiah 53, and (2) their history of political suppression.

Following the building of the temple, Alexander the Great took over world power from the Persians. (His activities helped spread Greek culture through the Middle East and East.) After he died, no single person was powerful enough to hold together the vast empire. A power struggle existed that lasted for years. Palestine lay between two forces of that struggle. The Ptolemies (from one of Alexander's generals, Ptolemy) controlled Egypt to the southwest of Palestine, while the Seleucids (from General Seleucius) controlled Syria to the north of Palestine.

Since Palestine lay between the two, it was a strategic place for both powers. They were constantly fighting each other. As the army of each would travel through Palestine, it would "practice on the Jews." At first the Ptolemies controlled Palestine. The Jews were their vassals, paying taxes to Egypt.

Eventually, the Seleucids took over Palestine. Things went better for the Jews until the Seleucids decided to become a world power and invaded Rome's territory to the west. Defeat resulted with tremendous military and monetary losses for the Seleucids. In fact, tribute money demanded by Rome was heavier than the Seleucids could pay.

Jason, one of the Jewish men, promised to pay a high sum to the Seleucid king, Antiochus IV, for the appointment of high priest. Antiochus agreed, and Jason forced Greek custom upon the Jews and unified the Jews to support Antiochus. Once the high priesthood (which by now was secularized as a combination of religious and civil leadership) was given to whomever would pay the most for it, the "musical chairs" began. Disunity and fighting became common among the Jews for this reason.

Finally, Antiochus decided the only way to keep trouble down in Palestine was to do away with the Jewish religion. He attempted to do so, but some Jews revolted (Maccabean revolt), and open war broke out. At one time the Jews defeated the Seleucids, took over Jerusalem, and restored the temple worship. For a short time, political independence was enjoyed. However, internal problems became so serious that the two opposing factions of the Jews asked Rome to intervene. After some hesitation, Rome did intervene but in a different way than expected. Rather than act as an arbitrator, it marched in to act as a conqueror. The immoral disunity among the Jews had again put them under foreign domination. Rome occupied the country with troops, kings, and governors.

Palestine was not free, but did not God promise a king like David would govern and increase the kingdom? Surely the time had come for the Christ (anointed king) to dethrone the Caesar. The Jews wanted a political king — and behold, a new star appeared in the sky! And the astrologers declared that a king had been born —the "king of the Jews." But He wasn't to head a kingdom of man. He was to initiate the kingdom of God!

Follow-up Questions

1. Describe "repentance." Use some particular sins in outlining evidence of repentance.

2. What then should happen prior to baptism?

3. In what ways does the church seek to be like those outside the church? Why does this happen?

4. Discuss the characteristics of God's new age. Where do you see this being fulfilled in the New Testament? Where do you see it being lived today?

5. Discuss how world political affairs affected the Jewish expectation for a Messiah. How do world political events today affect our concept of God? Of security? Of priorities? Of morality? Of honesty? Of compromise?

6. The Jewish revival in Babylon didn't last long. What should be done to help the results of any revival we experience to last and mature?

7. Discuss the significance of the Babylonian exile. What are some current events that have brought similar results? (Example: the POW's in Vietnam.)

Study Aid B

As it is important to read the Old Testament in its historical sequence, it is helpful to read the New Testament books in the light of the purpose of the authors. Space will not permit a comprehensive development of the purpose of each book, so I will merely suggest the major emphases for the reader to consider.

Matthew, Mark, Luke, and John are our major sources for the historical framework of Jesus' life. All four stress the crucifixion and resurrection. The total life of Jesus pointed to those events. Each Gospel book was written by a different man who had a different emphasis. The emphases were significant to the readers of the first century because of their setting in life and are of paramount importance to us.

Mark emphasized the deity of Christ as the Son of God. Matthew emphasized that Jesus was the Messiah promised in Jewish Scripture who came for the lost house of Israel. The Jewish rejection of Jesus was not His desire, but theirs. It was tied to their not keeping privilege and purpose together in their past history. John emphasized the reality of the new temple within man's body as God's dwelling place which God made possible through Jesus. Luke shows that Jesus is for *all* people, the universal Lord.

Acts continues where Luke left off to develop how the church historically crossed all barriers to include all kinds of people as participants in the kingdom of God. Luke, the author, is not developing the geographical expansion of Christianity, but its ethnical expansion.

In Galatians, Paul shows that no person is justified by the law but all people are justified by faith in Jesus Christ. In Romans, he expands that concept by showing the universality of sin and the universal salvation made possible in Christ plus its expression in society.

Paul answered specific questions in the Corinthian

and Thessalonian letters. In 1 Corinthians, he dealt primarily with problems they were having in the congregation. In the second letter (at least the second we have), we see the involvement of a loving leader. In the Thessalonian letters, he encouraged attitudes and corrected teachings.

Paul wrote in prison about the excellency of knowing God through Jesus (Colossians) and the unity created by responding with faith to that knowledge (Ephesians). He wrote about a practical application of that unity in Philemon. In Philippians, he called the members to live together as united citizens who manifest the characteristics of Christ.

First and 2 Timothy and Titus are called "pastoral epistles" (really all of Paul's letters are that) because Paul gave advice to men in performing their pastoral functions.

The writer of Hebrews emphasized that Jesus is the fulfillment of the Old Testament expectations and is thus superior to all that foreshadowed Him.

James; 1 and 2 Peter; 1, 2, and 3 John; and Jude are called "general epistles." These books emphasized how Christians are to apply their faith by practical care (James), by holy living amid an unholy environment (1 Peter), and by faithfulness amid falsehood (2 Peter). Jude warns against those who would threaten the unity of the Christian community. Third John commended a Christian who had remained faithful and expressed such in love; 2 John warned a Christian about indiscriminate fellowship; and 1 John gives guidelines for identifying a Christian.

In Revelation, John wrote a theology of hope reminding the Christians that God has victory both for their present trials and for their future times. Regardless of the external circumstances of gloom, God is still on His throne.

While Genesis shows us God at the beginning, Revelation shows us God at the end. "I am the Alpha and the Omega, the beginning and the end" (Revelation 21:6). History belongs to God — that is the message of Revelation and the entire Bible. Nowhere is it better stated than "the kingdom of the world has become the kingdom of our Lord, and of His Christ" (Revelation 11:15). It will be completed at the second coming of Christ; the book ends at the beginning point, "Yes, I am coming quickly" (Revelation 22:20). In the waiting period "the grace of the Lord Jesus be with all" (Revelation 22:21). Amen.

8

The King Comes

Birth

Even when Jesus was but a few days old, it was clear that He would usher in God's new age with its corresponding five characteristics that we have already introduced. That He was the Messiah (the Christ, the anointed one) is seen by the announcement to Mary, "He will be great, and will be called the Son of the Most High; and the Lord God will give Him the throne of His father David; and He will reign over the house of Jacob forever; and His kingdom will have no end" (Luke 1:32, 33). That He would die for humans to make forgiveness a reality is seen by the announcement, "You shall call His name Jesus, for it is He who will save His people from their sins" (Matthew 1:21), and the inspired announcement by Zacharias in Luke 1:77. That Jesus would initiate the new age of the Spirit is seen by the circumstances of His birth — conceived by the Holy Spirit (Matthew 1:20; Luke 1:35). That He would initiate justice and righteousness is apparent in the announcement of Mary in Luke 1:46-55. That this kingdom is for *all* peoples is seen by Simeon's announcement about Jesus, "Mine eyes have seen Thy salvation, which Thou hast prepared in the presence of all peoples, a light of revelation to the Gentiles, and the glory of Thy people Israel" (Luke 2:30-32). The term "all peoples" in Luke 2:31 is paralleled with "all flesh" in Luke 3:6, "All flesh shall see the salvation of God." These terms refer to the two ethnic groups that (in accordance with the Jewish mind) made up the entire population — Jews and Gentiles. Simeon defined "all peoples" as referring to Gentiles (v. 31) and to Israelites (v. 32). This point is very important, for it will help us to understand Acts 2:17, 39.

Both Jews and Gentiles witnessed Jesus' early infancy, the Jewish shepherds (Luke 2:8ff) and the Gentile magi (Matthew 2:1ff). Matthew emphasized that Jesus is the Messiah promised by the prophets. In the first three chapters of his book, he related Jeremiah, Isaiah, Micah, Hosea, and Malachi to Jesus. John the Baptist is the "Elijah" who was to prepare the way for the coming king (Matthew 3:1-3). Matthew compares the early life of Jesus with the sequence of the early life of Israel. As Israel went to Egypt as an infant-nation, so Jesus went to Egypt as an infant-person (Matthew 2:13-15). The God who called Israel out of Egypt called Jesus out of Egypt. Matthew applied to Jesus a passage from Hosea that was first applied to the nation — "Out of Egypt did I call My Son" (Hosea 11:1; Matthew 2:15). Israel was called God's first-born son just as Jesus was (see Exodus 4:22).

Baptism

After Israel came out of Egypt, it submitted to a baptism by passing through a body of water (see Paul's description in 1 Corinthians 10:1ff). The next event Matthew recorded in which Jesus participated was His submission to baptism (after He came out of Egypt). Luke recorded an incident in Jesus' boyhood days, but Matthew wanted to maintain the relationship of Jesus with Israel by tracing His human genealogy no further back than to Abraham, the father of Israel. Since Luke developed the concept that Jesus is Lord of all, he traced Jesus' genealogy all the way back to Adam.

The baptism of Jesus is very significant, for it is God's public coronation of Jesus as king and at the same time His ordination as a servant or minister. His coronation as king is evident by both God's action and His words. His action was the public anointing with the Holy Spirit. The dove coming upon Jesus served as that objective anointing act. Peter referred to this baptism as God's anointing of Jesus (Acts 10:38). God's words, "This is My beloved Son" (Matthew 3:17), also bear out the coronation as king. Those words were recorded in Psalm 2, a psalm spoken at the coronation of Jewish kings. That the baptism was also Jesus' ordination for ministry is apparent by God's next words, "In whom I am well-pleased" (Matthew 3:17) and by Jesus' first sermon (Luke 4:16-21). This second phrase was a Messianic phrase recorded in Isaiah 42:1. However, this last phrase was never spoken at a king's coronation. The passage in Isaiah began a long series of passages on the suffering servant. These passages reach a climax in Isaiah 53 that speaks about a death-sacrifice. God declared that His king is to be a suffering servant-king. He is not to be the political hero some Jews were expecting.

From this time on, Jesus lived out the role of a servant-king. He served men under God and thus re-established a theocracy, the kingdom of God. Immediately after His baptism, He went into the wilderness, as did the Israelites (Exodus 15:22ff), for the purpose of serving God (Exodus 5:1-3). As the Israelites were tested in their wilderness experience, so was Jesus; however, He did not handle His temptation the way they did. They did not believe in God's sufficiency; Jesus did. They wanted to return and serve the Egyptians; Jesus wanted to serve God. Every answer Jesus gave to Satan was a quote from Moses (Matthew 4:4, see Deuteronomy 8:3; Matthew 4:7, see Deuteronomy 6:16; Matthew 4:10, see Deuteronomy 6:13). It is important that the church study these temptations thoroughly, for Satan constantly keeps them before God's people.

First Temptation (Matthew 4:3, 4)

Jesus could have heard the first temptation (turn stones to bread) as an avenue to ministry. After all, if He could not stay alive, how could He minister to the needs of others? In performing this miracle, He could gain a sizable following in a short time. Who would not follow a leader who could provide the material things people needed? Jesus knew that many expected the Messiah to usher in an abundance of material goods (Isaiah 49:10). Jesus' answer came from Moses' farewell address to Israel in which he rehearsed the acts of God. Moses indicated that God let the Israelites hunger in the wilderness to teach them dependence on God. The theme of Deuteronomy 8:3ff is that the Israelites should not forget the chief provider — God, who brought them out of slavery (Deuteronomy 8:14) and who provides the necessities (Deuteronomy 8:9). If they forget, they will die (Deuteronomy 8:20). Jesus was tempted to forget God as were the Israelites. "Take the situation into your own hands" is the suggestion of Satan. But Jesus' answer made it apparent that He had learned the lesson that Israel had not — God will provide.

Jesus knew that the role of a lasting ministry did not come by putting self first. Jesus perceived that the need of humanity was not to turn stones into bread, but souls into brothers, and that a following brought about by the aroma of fresh bread would be temporary.

This same temptation faces the "body of Christ" today. "Stay alive, church" is a pressing mandate. Our church buildings are expensive and are big investments, so we must have financial food or we will die. It may be tempting to change stones (closed pocketbooks) into bread (offerings) by catering to the expectations of the people or by allowing them to write our curriculum in order to insure that they will write their checks. We must not be the protectors of society's status quo. We must seek to substitute the desire for the perpetuation of self for the desire for a ministry to others. This calls for dependence upon the lordship of God. It calls for obedience to the prophets and the redemptive mission of God's anointed people. It calls for a remembrance of the One who brought us out of slavery and through the waters.

May the church not present a false presence of the kingdom by catering to the expectations (in teaching or actions) of the kingdoms of men — whether political or social kingdoms. The church's place is in the wilderness with the stones all around her. If they are to change, it must be God's doing through the humbling obedience of the church.

Second Temptation (Matthew 4:5-7)

In this temptation, Satan suggested that Jesus use sensationalism as a means to get a following — after all, there is nothing impossible with God! It would fit in with popular expectations. Certainly Psalm 91:11 provided the necessary protection: "Can you really trust Psalm 91:11, Jesus?" the tempter asked.

Jesus' answer was again from Moses' farewell address (Deuteronomy 6:16) in which he referred to Israel's test of God at Massah to prove God's existence to them. Moses called them to an essential trust instead of an extraordinary test (Deuteronomy 6:17). Jesus knew that the demand of a sensational test indicated a lack of sincere trust in God, so He could not do it. Furthermore, He knew that it would encourage men to follow magic rather than the Master. God's claims did not need continual sensationalism. Moses told the people that the object of their faith must be such that when asked by their children the reason for it, they could answer, "God — He brought us out from there in order to bring us in" (Deuteronomy 6:23).

The same temptation faces the "body of Christ" today. We, too, are tempted to continually seek signs as did God's old Israel (1 Corinthians 1:22). We are tempted to seek some sensational manifestation of God's spirit as proof that God accepts us. In doing this we bypass His primary manifestation — the resurrection (1 Peter 1:3ff). Israel's problem was that it did not believe the promises of God (Psalm 106:24) and so had to have sensational sign after sensational sign. Jesus will not trust himself to a people like that (John 2:23ff). We have seen enough of God's faithfulness to His word that His word is all the assurance we should need. He was tested at the cross. Isn't that enough proof that He loves us? And isn't that what we are to preach (1 Corinthians 1:23)? Isn't that the power of God to save anyone (Romans 1:16; 1 Corinthians 1:24)? The church dare not dangle the magnetism of the sensational before people instead of the power of the cross. We must not be hard-pressed for an answer when asked by our children the reason for our faith. May our faith not rest upon the sensations of men but upon the salvation of God.

Third Temptation (Matthew 4:8-10)

Following the coronation announcement in Psalm 2:7, which was spoken at Jesus' baptism by God, is the promise, "Ask of Me, and I will surely give the nations as Thy inheritance, and the very ends of the earth as Thy possession" (Psalm 2:8). The Messiah was to redeem the world. Satan offered a way to get the world on a silver platter, so it seemed. The temptation was to bypass God's way for an easier and quicker route. It was to bypass God's announced way for a successful kingship (1 Samuel 12:14ff). Satan had used this on every king of the Jews before Jesus with extremely great success.

Jesus' answer came from Deuteronomy 6:10ff in which Moses warned the people not to forget God who was responsible for their redemption (v. 12). He told them not to go after other gods (v. 14), or the Lord would surely destroy them (v. 15). Their way was to be God's way as they lived out their lives in service. There was to be no shortcut. But old Israel did not heed. The kings forgot God and led the people astray. But Jesus knew that His kingship was not to gain the world unto himself, but to bring men to His Father. And He knew that a humanity obtained without demands from it and without its own voluntary commitment would be an unredeemed humanity.

This temptation is ours today. Matthew 28:19, 20 rings in our ears: "Make disciples of all the nations." We talk of worldwide missions and desire worldwide success. The gleam is in our eyes. We often use quantity only to measure progress. How to increase numbers is a question we all face, for numbers are important. One way is the same way offered to Jesus: "Don't demand too much. Give in a little to evil; learn to compromise. Depend upon the power the world uses to force the populace to her knees." The former kings had followed that route, and so had Israel.

The church must understand these three temptations well. What appears to be appealing for survival and success is the means to destruction. Old Israel was hoodwinked and forfeited her role as God's servant by catering to these same three temptations. We must not follow suit by catering to worldly popularity, sensationalism, and compromise. What way is left? It is the same way that was left for Jesus — the way of the cross. It is the way of lowly service, personal involvement, hard work, shame, self-denial, radical trust in God, and death.

In His testings, Jesus reversed the attitudes of the Israelites. At the outset, He showed that He was determined not to go the route of an autonomous *man*archy, but rather the route of submission to a theocracy. He would be God's righteous king who would speak only what He had heard the Father speak (John 3:34; 7:16; 8:28) and would perform the Father's activities (John 5:19). His life would be lived in total accordance to God's will (John 5:30; Matthew 26:39). As a king, He would follow the only way God outlined that a kingship would work (1 Samuel 12:14ff). What the Israelites rejected, Jesus accepted. No wonder John the Baptist declared before Jesus came that "the kingdom of heaven is at hand" (Matthew 3:2; Mark 1:15). But Jesus could declare, "The kingdom of God is in your midst" (Luke 17:21).

May the world see the church today continuing in His way — the way of lowly service that will demonstrate to the world that God is love. May the church not only pray but demonstrate, "Thy kingdom come. Thy will be done, on earth as it is in heaven."

Follow-up Questions

1. Discuss the significance of Jesus' baptism.

2. How does the church try to turn closed pocketbooks into offerings? Why?

3. What are the pros and cons to the use of sensationalism? What should be the purpose and limitation of their use? What are some sensational methods we use to get a crowd?

4. What are some compromises tempting us today?

5. Does self-survival and growth necessarily indicate God's will is being done? Discuss.

9

The King Acts

Jesus knew that He was the Messiah, but He also knew that God had called Him to head a new Israel and not just to be an individual redeemer. Therefore, His first act after the baptism-temptation experience was to initiate fellowship with four men who would later become students, traveling and living with Him (John 1:35ff). Our vertical relationship with God must always be followed by our horizontal relationship with men of God. Jesus cannot give the command to love God without including the command to love our fellowmen (Matthew 22:37-40).

Immediately, Jesus began to live out God's will as both king and servant in what He said and did. Both His words and activities revealed His nature. When John's disciples asked Him sometime later if He were the Christ, Jesus replied, "Go and report to John the things which you hear and see" (Matthew 11:4). These two expressions, words and deeds, complement one another. What Jesus said interpreted what He did, and what He did explained the meaning of much that He said. Both served to reveal to humanity what God is like. Jesus made visible the invisible God (Colossians 1:15) by reflecting the character of God's nature (Hebrews 1:3). He was God (John 1:1; 1 John 5:20; Colossians 2:9) who had put on flesh (John 1:14; Philippians 2:5ff). When we see both kingship and servanthood in Jesus, we are to know that God is both lord and servant. Jesus said, "He who has seen Me has seen the Father" (John 14:9). God has been man's serving lord from the creation.

Throughout all Jesus' life we can see either His king (lord) or His servant role being manifested. His first miracle showed that He is lord of nature as He turned some water into wine (John 2:1-11). His first act after that (cleansing the temple) illustrated that He had come to initiate the "new age" God had promised. While the Jews believed that God's house was the temple where God lived in only one room, Jesus promised a new temple — the temple of His body (John 2:13-22). God intended from creation that He live in the hearts of men (Genesis 2:7). Men were to be His earthly temple. At the very beginning of Jesus' ministry, He declared the event that would make that possible — His death and resurrection (John 2:19).

His next teaching session stressed the possibility of the new life in the kingdom of God. A man must experience a new birth (John 3:5). The new life is the life of the Spirit (John 6:63; 7:37-39; Romans 7:6; 1 Corinthians 15:45; 2 Corinthians 3:6). Jesus taught that the availability of the Spirit would be possible because of His death (John 3:14, 15). God's motivation was behind it (John 3:16).

As Jesus left Judea, the place of His baptism and first miracle, He stressed again that a new day would come when people would worship God in Spirit (John 4:24) and promised that He could give that Spirit (John 4:14; relate to John 7:38ff). As He came close to His hometown, He showed that He was lord over life by healing the official's son (John 4:46ff).

Coronation Speech

Jesus told His hometown friends the platform for the expected Messiah. In the sermon in His hometown synagogue, He read from Isaiah 61:1: "The Spirit of the Lord is upon Me, because He anointed Me to preach the gospel to the poor. He has sent Me to proclaim release to the captives, and recovery of sight to the blind, to set free those who are downtrodden, to proclaim the favorable year of the Lord" (Luke 4:18, 19).

That prophecy in Isaiah referred to the suffering servant-king.

Jesus continued, "Today this Scripture has been fulfilled in your hearing" (Luke 4:21). He was telling them that the King had come and was with them, but the people did not catch on at first. Nor did they catch the impact of the activities listed in that Isaiah passage. They did not take the Scripture literally as God meant it or as Jesus lived it. The poor, the captives, the blind, and the oppressed were the neglected people in Israel. False, human-made barriers had kept them in their places. Jewish leaders did little to cross those barriers.

God is love, but few knew it at the start of the first century. Therefore, God decided to come in person to demonstrate His love (John 1:18) and to pour His kind of love into man's heart (John 17:26; Romans 5:5; Galatians 5:22; John 13:34; 1 Corinthians 13). God's coming in Christ was "to proclaim the favorable year of the Lord" (Luke 4:19). This was referring to the year of Jubilee which was a year of redemption when slaves would be set free. They would no longer be forsaken (Isaiah 62:4), for God himself would visit them in flesh on this earth. But Jesus' hometown friends did not understand that God in Jesus intended to cross and crush the barriers that had separated man from his fellowman. That was not the Christ they expected, nor the Christ they wanted.

Jesus sensed that the people did not understand that He would shatter traditions and cross barriers, so He gave two examples from history that demonstrated that God in the past loved and cared for people who were outside Judaism. Jesus told of how Elijah was not sent to an Israelite widow during the famine, but God sent him to a widow in the land of Sidon. He told of Elisha cleansing a leper from Syria, enemies of the Jews, rather than any Israelite leper (Luke 4:25-27). Jesus did not use Elijah and Elisha without purpose, for the Jews had associated the forerunner of the Messiah as a type of Elijah and Christ as a type of Elisha.

The people suddenly got the point, for immediately upon hearing this they were filled with anger and tried to kill Jesus. God's program of love will always be opposed by man's prejudices of hate. Again we see the difference between the kingdom of God and the kingdom of man.

Actions Follow His Words

Jesus immediately began to live out the promises in that coronation speech. He cast out an unclean demon (Luke 4:31-37) and touched a sick person to heal her (Luke 4:38, 39). In these acts, He showed His kingship (Lord over nature) and His servanthood (He ministered to their needs). He crossed barriers others would not cross, and people of every kind came to Him (Luke 4:40).

Throughout His life, He met both the physical and the spiritual needs of people. When will we learn that, as Christ's body today, we are to meet the needs of the people all about us? We, too, are to love the unlovely and touch the untouchable. If we would do more crossing of barriers, perhaps people would come to us. Is it right that He who was holy was called the friend of sinners, while we who bear His name are not? We are not to act above our Master (John 13:16).

Jesus continued His ministry showing that He is the kind of Lord who uses His lordship to serve the needs of the people. His privilege was coupled with purpose, His exaltation with humility, His power with pity, His superiority with sacrifice. He broke ritual traditions to meet the needs of people. He permitted His disciples to pick grain on the Sabbath (Luke 6:1-5; Mark 2:23-28; Matthew 12:1-8). He himself worked on the Sabbath to help others (Matthew 12:9-14; Mark 3:1-6; Luke 6:6-11; John 5:1-9) and made it clear that God does also (John 5:17). His disciples did not keep all the religious practices just because it had always been done that way (Matthew 15:1ff; Mark 7:1ff). He touched a leper (Matthew 8:1-4; Mark 1:40ff; Luke 5:12-16) and material that a dead person had touched (Luke 7:11-17), both of which made Him religiously "unclean" according to tradition.

He forgave the "unforgivables" of His day — a woman rejected by religious leaders (Luke 7:36-50), a woman caught in adultery (John 8:1-11), an exploiter of people (Luke 19:2-10), an unknown "commoner" (Matthew 9:1-8; Mark 2:1-12; Luke 5:17-27), the disciples who denied Him, and His own executioners (Luke 23:34). And when Jesus forgives, He forgets (Hebrews 8:12).

He was not threatened by broad associations. He could include a diversity of vocations in His inner group (fishermen to tax collector) and a diversity of political philosophies (Zealot against Rome, Simon; and an employee of the Roman system, Matthew). He could associate with men and women, young and old, well and sick, rich and poor. He could have dinner with religious leaders (Matthew 15:1ff), wealthy exploiters (Luke 19:1-10), and the community riff-raff (Luke 15:1, 2). He was not embarrassed to be seen with any of them.

His ministry of care was not restricted to His own group nor to those who would necessarily follow Him. He neither counted the cost nor had a guarantee of a positive return. He helped a widow in her lonely grief (Luke 7:11-17), a woman in her frustration of not being well to serve her guests (Matthew 8:14, 15), a man whose friends cared (Matthew 9:2-8), and a man who did not even ask for help (Matthew 12:9-14). He helped a man everyone ostracized into a solitary life (Matthew 8:28-34), a crowd of hungry people (Matthew 14:13-21; 15:32-38; Mark 6:32-44; Luke 9:10-17; John 6:1-14), a woman of a despised race (Matthew

15:21-28), and a convicted criminal (Luke 23:39-43).

He was demonstrating to the world the kind of Creator and Lord this world has. He reversed what old Israel had done. No wonder the very ones old Israel had alienated came seeking Jesus (John 12:20, 21). He called twelve men (Matthew 10:2-4) to become the first members of the new Israel (Galatians 6:10), the extended body of Christ (Ephesians 1:23; Colossians 1:18), so that what God began to do in Jesus might be continued by His followers. (Starting with twelve apostles upon which the foundation of the new Israel is built — Ephesians 2:20 — is another way that Jesus' early ministry has parallels with old Israel which was built upon twelve tribes.) Jesus' kind of ministry is to be ours (John 17:18). We dare not build or maintain the fences He came to cross. As Jesus lived out the love of God, He spoke His most neglected (by us) beatitude, "Blessed is he who keeps from stumbling over Me" (Luke 7:23). May we be so blessed!

Follow-up Questions

1. In what ways has the church succeeded or failed to live out the implications of Jesus' coronation speech?

2. What barriers between people has your congregation not often crossed? Race? Class? Education? Age? Which do you avoid?

3. Who are the people in your community most neglected by the church? What can we do for these people?

4. List physical needs Jesus met. List spiritual needs. Do we tend to emphasize one over the other?

5. What customs or traditions stand in the way of our meeting the needs of people? Would you miss a worship service to help someone?

6. Relate James 1:27 and Isaiah 1:11-15 to Jesus' kind of life.

10

The King Teaches

Jesus not only lived a life under God's kingdom, but also taught God's kingdom (Matthew 4:17; Mark 1:15; Acts 1:3). In both ways He communicated what it means to live under God's kingdom.

He taught that God's kingdom does not begin in external practices but in internal principles. God's kingdom begins with thinking, but so does the kingdom of man. Murder begins in hating, adultery in lusting, worship in selflessness (Matthew 5:21ff; 6:1ff). Purity or defilement are first determined by what is in a man (Matthew 15:11; 23:25-28; Mark 7:15-23).

New Love

Jesus taught that the total law-system of Judaism was fulfilled in love. When asked about the greatest commandment, He replied, " 'You shall love the Lord your God with all your heart, and with all your soul, and with all your mind.' . . . And a second is like it, 'You shall love your neighbor as yourself.' On these two commandments depend the whole Law and the Prophets" (Matthew 22:37-40; Mark 12:30, 31; Luke 10:27; relate to Romans 13:8; Galatians 5:14ff).

All of His teaching and activities further illustrate those statements. There are many important truths to notice about them: (1) The love is expressed in three directions — upward to God, inward to self, and outward to others. Love must be expressed in that order, for unless one loves and accepts God, He will not love and accept himself. Unless one loves and accepts himself, he will not love and accept others.

(2) The love discussed here is love — *agape* style. *Agape*-love means that a person lives unselfishly for

others. That kind of love was God's motivation in helping man (John 3:16; Romans 5:8), and it is to be the motivation of His church. The moment a church fails to tackle a need because of the cost, the worth of the person with the need, or certain anticipated benefits that might not return to the church, it fails to act with the motivation of the Creator.

(3) The neighbor is anyone with a need, as seen in Jesus' parable of the good Samaritan. To *be* a neighbor is to meet another's need (Luke 10:29-37).

(4) The law is fulfilled by living in God's way. It is love-living. This gives us one purpose of the law. It was God's way of defining the content of love. God who designed persons knows what is best for them. His commandments are for our good.

However, by the time Jesus came to earth, the love-intent of the law had been ignored by the traditions Jewish scholars had added to the law. Property had taken priority over people and customs over care. Jesus taught that any "religious" tradition that intervened with the love-intent of the law transgresses the law, "Why do you yourselves transgress the commandment of God for the sake of your tradition?" (Matthew 15:3). In fact, some traditions muzzled and/or rejected the law (Matthew 15:56; Mark 7:8-13)). It has always been easy to become more zealous about perpetuating traditions of men than practicing love to them (Galatians 1:14; Romans 10:2, 3).

Since many traditions obscured the love-purpose of God, God came to earth in flesh saying, "Here is what it means to love." Jesus taught that God was primarily concerned about people, not programs (Matthew 23:1-7). He told the religious program-oriented leaders on two occasions, "Go and learn what this means, 'I desire compassion, and not sacrifice' " (Matthew 9:13; 12:7). And He taught some applications of that truth: (1) Worship should be preceded by reconciliation with brothers (Matthew 5:23, 24). (2) Practicing commandments without genuine care for others is a facade (Matthew 19:16-22). (3) The happy person is the merciful person (Matthew 5:7). (4) A man's neglect of the needy will condemn him (Luke 16:19-31; Romans 12:6-8). (5) His instruction to those He sent out included not just preaching, but ministering to physical needs (Matthew 10:5-8; Mark 6:7-13). (6) Evangelizing was to be followed by teaching *all* Jesus commanded (Matthew 28:19, 20).

New Attitudes

Jesus taught that this kind of kingdom action required kingdom attitudes. It called for radical trust in the provisions of God (Matthew 6:33, 34). It called for a denial of selfishness (Matthew 16:24; Mark 8:34-38; Luke 9:23-26). It called for the giving up of prejudices (Matthew 5:43-48). It called for the humble attitude of servanthood (Matthew 20:20-28; 23:11; Mark 10:24-31; relate to Philippians 2:3-11; John 13:1-20). Values must be reversed — love for the will of God must stand over a love for family (Luke 14:26; the word "hate" in this text means to give someone second place. It does not mean to despise; it is only when we give God first place that we can really love the family as we should), and over commitment to accepted social customs (Matthew 8:21, 22).

New Source

Putting it simply, kingdom attitudes call for nothing short of a new life which is what Jesus taught (John 3). He was not only that new life himself (John 14:6; 5:26), but also He came to make it possible for all to participate in that new life (John 10:10). Since that life is himself, we must receive Him to have it (John 1:12; 3:36; 5:40; 6:27, 35, 47, 54; 8:12; 10:28; 14:6). The purpose for writing the Gospel of John was that we might believe in Jesus and participate in this eternal life (20:31). The word "eternal" does not imply just duration (forever), but also quality (good).

The Spirit who equipped Jesus to love can live in people. As Jesus was the temple of God, so can individuals be. Jesus died in order to make that possible. On the night of His betrayal, He drew together an understanding of what His life had been about, and what His death would be about. During the Lord's Supper, He portrayed His life when He took the function of a slave and washed His apostles' feet (John 13:1-17). When Simon Peter finally agreed to the action of Jesus and asked that Jesus wash all of him, Jesus refused. The rest of Peter's body did not need washing (John 13:10). Only his feet needed it because of the dusty roads and his habit of wearing sandals. Jesus was saying that He was not interested in being busy just for activity's sake. The church must learn this lesson. There is no New Testament teaching that suggests that the church calendar *has* to be full for growth of the church.

Jesus then shared a great commission with His apostles, "A new commandment I give to you, that you love one another, even as I have loved you, that you also love one another. By this all men will know that you are My disciples, if you have love for one another" (John 15:34, 35).

Jesus talks about going away; He is not referring primarily to Heaven, but to the cross (John 13:33), for on the cross He will prepare a place for them (John 14:2). What kind of place? The context of John 14—17 (really all of John) suggests that the place Jesus is describing is an earthly place. He died to prepare the hearts of men to receive the Holy Spirit; when the hearts of men receive the Spirit, their bodies will be God's new temple.

While the Jews taught that God lived in only one room of the temple, Jesus taught, "In My Father's house are many dwelling places" (John 14:2). "My Father's house" is a term applied to the temple in Jewish terminology (John 2:16; Matthew 21:13; Luke 19:45, 46; see and relate Isaiah 56:7; Jeremiah 7:11). Before the temple was built, the term was used to refer to the dwelling place of God on earth. The term was never used to speak about God's *heavenly* dwelling place, but always about His earthly dwelling place. The many "rooms" are the lives of men; this is made clearer in John 14:23, "We will come and make our room with him" (original translation). This is the same word for room that is used in 14:2 and probably refers to the same promise. Paul later called the individual body of a Christian, God's temple (1 Corinthians 6:19). Each regenerated person is a dwelling place for God and is added to all the other "rooms" to make up the total earthly new temple of God (1 Corinthians 3:16; Ephesians 2:19-22; relate concept of "house" in Hebrews 3:6 and 1 Peter 2:5).

Jesus wanted the apostles to know that as God's Spirit lived in Him enabling Him to love, the Spirit will also live in them. In John 14:16, He promised another *paraclete* (counselor, comforter, helper). The word "another" here means another *just like* Jesus. The *paraclete* is referred to as the Spirit (v. 17), and as Jesus (v. 18), and as the combination of the Father and the Son (v. 23). All this suggests that the Spirit is the historical presence of the complete Godhead (Father, Son, and Holy Spirit). It is only when we are united to Christ through the Spirit that we are united to God (Ephesians 2:18) and that we can bear fruit (John 15). The fruit in John 15 is primarily the fruit of loving as Jesus loved (vv. 8, 9, 12, 13). The promise of the Spirit in chapter 14, the emphasis on love in chapter 15, the expanded teaching about the Spirit in chapter 16, and the prayer asking for that unity in chapter 17 which ends on the note of love (v. 26), together with the command in

John 13:34, 35 show that the fruit of love comes from the Holy Spirit which unites us to God who is love.

It is the Spirit of God that produces *agape*-love in people (Romans 5:5; Galatians 5:22; 2 Timothy 1:7; Romans 14:17). But sin separates men from that Spirit. That is why the world was so unlovely when Jesus came.

Then the king submitted himself to His greatest act of love. He took man's sin as His own. We are able to love because of that act of His love (1 John 4:9-11). He went to the cross to prepare a place for us. Only when we allow God to dwell in us here will we dwell with Him there. Get ready for a new life which is where God's kingdom begins.

Follow-up Questions

1. Discuss whether or not property is taking priority over people today. Will we go into as much debt to help people in need as we will to build buildings? Why do some groups spend more money on interest payments than on missionary work?

2. Are we program-oriented or people-oriented?

3. In one column list the activities that are done in the church building around meetings. In another column, list activities done outside the church building in service to people. What does your listing reveal?

4. What are the implications of being the temple of God?

5. Compare John 1:18 and 1 John 4:12.

11

The King Died, Yet Lives

Jesus' Commitment

After Jesus finished giving His apostles the commandment to love as He loved and explaining that it would be possible when the Spirit came to unite men with God (John 13:34 — 16:33), and after praying for the reality of this unity (John 17), He and His apostles went to the Garden of Gethsemane (Matthew 26:36ff; Mark 14:32ff; Luke 22:39ff; John 18:1ff).

As His earthly ministry opened in the midst of temptations designed to detour Him from His mission, it closed in the same manner. For each time He declared to Satan in the wilderness that He would follow God, He declared to God in this garden, "Not my will, but thine be done." Nevertheless, He did ask that the cup He was about to taste be removed from Him if it was possible (Matthew 26:39, 42, 44).

The "cup" was the kind of death that He was about to taste. It was not just a physical death; it was also the essential death — a separation from the Father. By praying, "If it be possible," He meant that if man's unity with God could become a reality in any other way, then He could bypass tasting the separation-death (Hebrews 2:9). But there was no other way, for sin had separated man from God's Spirit and had brought that essential death to every man who had sinned (Romans 5:12). The eternal Jesus entered into the temporal world to accept man's sin as His own and receive unto himself the consequences of that sin — separation from the Father.

The Meaning of His Death

The Bible interprets His death in this way: "Behold, the Lamb of God who takes away the sin of the world!"

(John 1:29); "Christ our passover also has been sacrificed" (1 Corinthians 5:7); "Christ ... having been offered once to bear the sins of many" (Hebrews 9:28). Christ offered a single sacrifice of himself for sin (Hebrews 10:11, 12). He himself became the sin-offering (Isaiah 53:10; Romans 8:3). Sins were laid on Him as they were symbolically laid on animals of old Israel. But now symbol had turned into reality. Those animals had to be without blemish, as was Christ (Hebrews 9:14). "He was pierced through for our transgressions, He was crushed for our iniquities.... The Lord has caused the iniquity of us all to fall on Him" (Isaiah 53:5, 6). For our sake, God made Jesus to be sin (2 Corinthians 5:21). Christ became a curse for us (Galatians 3:13). "He Himself bore our sins in His body on the cross" (1 Peter 2:24).

This substitutionary death brought ransom, redemption, reconciliation, a new creation, and righteousness to man. Jesus gave His life as a ransom (Mark 10:45) which purchased us for God. That ransom redeemed us (Galatians 4:5; Hebrews 9:15). The basic idea of redemption is liberation. His death released us from the slavery to sin (Colossians 1:13; Ephesians 1:7) to the freedom of enjoying a renewed fellowship with God (1 John 1:3). His death served as the only possibility for man's reconciliation with God (Colossians 1:20; Romans 5:10; Ephesians 2:16; 2 Corinthians 5:18). Reconciliation is accompanied by the renewal of the Holy Spirit who produces a new creation (Titus 3:5; 2 Corinthians 5:17; John 3). This renewal makes righteousness possible (Isaiah 53:11; Romans 3:21-26; 5:18, 19; 6:3, 4; 14:17; 1 Corinthians 1:30; 2 Corinthians 5:21; Philippians 3:9; 1 Peter 2:24).

Righteousness is possible only by God's act of justification. The Bible makes it apparent that "justification" has two sides to it — acquittal and equipment. The acquittal is God's verdict of "not guilty" that God declares to us because Jesus took our guilt. God not only declares us innocent if we accept Christ, but He also does what no human judge can do in any law court — He gives to us the ability to live a life of righteousness. That equipment is His own Spirit (Ephesians 1:13, 14; 2 Corinthians 1:21, 22; John 14 — 16). Peter's promise in Acts 2:38 makes apparent the two aspects of justification. No wonder the Christ is described as the power and wisdom of God (1 Corinthians 1:24), the news of whom can bring about an obedience of faith (Romans 1:4, 5).

Knowing that the wages of sin is death (Romans 6:23) and that that kind of death is alienation from the Father, Jesus was willing to accept man's sin as His own in order to remove the barrier of alienation between man and God. To do so meant that the same barrier would be placed between Jesus and the heavenly Father. It was that cup He did not want to taste and that made Him sorrowful (Matthew 26:38; Mark 14:34). Nevertheless, out of His love for humanity, He did it to make reconciliation possible between man and God. (For description of the alienation-death see Ephesians 2:1, 12.)

He Died

The temptation to bypass the cross continued until the end. The apostles wanted to bypass the cross by fighting, but Jesus refused (Matthew 26:50-56). For fear they might also be assigned to a cross, they fled (Matthew 26:56). Jesus could have done that; on several threatening occasions, He fled rather miraculously (e.g. Luke 4:29, 30). Jesus also was tempted to rationalize His way out, but He refused (Matthew 26:62ff; 27:12; Mark 15:4, 5; John 18:36). He was no doubt tempted to take personal retaliation, but He would not (Matthew 26:67; Mark 14:65; Luke 22:63-65; John 19:1-3; Matthew 27:27-30; Mark 15:16-19). He was tempted to take drugs so that His senses might be dulled, but He refused (Matthew 27:34; Mark 15:33). He would not allow anything to stand in the way of His loving, voluntary, and willing decision.

While Jesus refused to yield to the temptations of the devil, others did not. As already mentioned, the apostles yielded to the temptation of self-security. The accusers yielded to the temptation of envy (Matthew 27:18), falsehood (Matthew 26:59-61), political engineering (John 19:12), mob agitation (Matthew 27:23-25), and of reversing social justice (Matthew 27:26). They chose to free a life-taker rather than the Life-giver (Luke 23:25). And while the Jewish people were sanctioning all this dishonesty, envy, and hatred, they kept their ritual purity to the letter. They would not enter Pilate's chambers in order to avoid becoming ritually unclean (by entering a Gentile's quarters); Pilate had to go in and out (note the times Pilate does this from John 18:28 — 19:16).

While others were concerned only about themselves, Jesus was concerned about others to the end. His last words as well as His last act before His death showed His care for others. He was concerned about the welfare of His accusers and executioners (Luke 23:34), of a criminal (Luke 23:43), and of His mother (John 19:25-27). His final words expressed His ultimate love for *all* humanity, "My God why hast Thou forsaken Me?" (Matthew 27:46; Mark 15:34) and "It is finished" (John 19:30).

Why did He feel He was forsaken? He was accepting unto himself the alienation that belonged to sinful men. We dare not dilute this significance of the death of Jesus on the cross. He tasted spiritual death for every man (Hebrews 2:9); not physical death, for regenerated men will continue to die physically. Our bodies are mortal.

The destruction of the works of the devil (for which Jesus had come) had been accomplished (1 John 3:8) when Jesus declared, "It is finished." Sin had been condemned (Romans 8:3); the ruler of the world (Satan) was judged (John 16:11). The barrier that had existed between God and man had been removed, thus the veil in the temple that had kept people from entering into the presence of God was torn asunder (Luke 23:45). The possibility of a sinful humanity reconciled to God and experiencing the renewal of the Holy Spirit (John 14—17; Titus 3:5) had become a reality. In Christ's death, God forgave man's sin, and no further offering for sin will be needed (Hebrews 10:18).

However, man must accept that forgiveness. God will not force reconciliation upon those who do not want renewed fellowship with God. Man has earned his wages for sin, but God will offer His gift as a lover (Romans 6:23).

Appropriation to Us

Man must also experience a voluntary death. He must voluntarily die to selfishness, turn from his sins, and confess Jesus as Savior and Lord. He must be willing to be led by the Holy Spirit not just receive the Spirit. This is the personal application of Jesus' death. Jesus died so that man *could* die to self and live to God (Romans 6; 2 Corinthians 5:14). "He died for all, that they who live should no longer live for themselves, but for Him who died and rose again on their behalf" (2 Corinthians 5:15). As Jesus denied himself on the cross, man must also deny his selfishness on his cross. What is man's cross? It is the crucifixion of His autonomous, individualistic living that is shattered as he sees the love of God displayed on the cross and falls in love with that God and trusts Him. He then expresses that shattering of self-mastery in a baptism that appropriates Christ's death to the self (Romans 6). Jesus referred to His cross as a baptism to make this connection clear (Mark 10:38; Luke 12:50).

Have we made baptism more of a ritual than of a

self-crucifixion? Has it become more of a "guarantee for Heaven" than a self-confession that a sinner is voluntarily being buried into Christ's kind of death and that he intends to live unselfishly for others as Jesus continued to do? Have we made it more of an entrance into a membership than into a Master (Romans 7:4; 1 Corinthians 12:12, 13)?

Let us not teach the mode with more emphasis than we teach the reason. Let us not relate it more to symbol than to Spirit. If there is no repentance or a crucifixion of self, the baptism will be of no spiritual effect — none whatsoever. "Water regeneration" is not taught in the Bible; but "Spirit regeneration" is taught, and it will not occur unless a voluntary death of self takes place. I'm afraid we speak more about the burial than about the death. I fear that we relate forgiveness of sins more to baptism than we relate the Holy Spirit to it. Consequently, many never know that the Spirit is living within them. What a pity that ritualism has taken its toll among us.

Each person must climb onto the cross with Jesus and participate in the denial of selfishness and sin if he intends to participate in Jesus' kind of life (study carefully Romans 6:3—8:39; Galatians 3:34—4:31). Only a voluntary crucifixion is followed by a spiritual resurrection. It is then that selfishness is replaced by true selfhood—that is what it means to be in the image of God.

Yet He Lives

As important as the death of Jesus is, it has little significance without the resurrection. However, His death and resurrection without the kind of life Jesus lived has no more relevance for us than the death and resurrection of Lazarus (John 11:1-44). This point is made clear in those passages that speak about His death as an offering for sin. He "knew no sin" (2 Corinthians

5:21); He "committed no sin" (1 Peter 2:22). "He had done no violence nor was there any deceit in His mouth" (Isaiah 53:9). He was without blemish (Hebrews 9:14); He was tempted in every possible way any man is (Hebrews 2:18) but without sinning (Hebrews 4:15). He was perfect (Hebrews 5:9), "holy, innocent, undefiled" (Hebrews 7:26); thus He had no need to offer sacrifices for His own sins (Hebrews 7:27). What is my point? If Jesus had sinned himself, His death could not have been a substitutionary death for us. It would have been His own deserved separation-death.

What would be an objective proof that the apostles were correct in their reports that He was without sin? That proof is in the resurrection of Jesus. Had Jesus been guilty of sin, He would not have arisen from the grave never to die again (Lazarus died again). The resurrection declares to us that in His death our sins were forgiven. Paul pointed this out when he wrote, "If Christ has not been raised, your faith is worthless; you are still in your sins" (1 Corinthians 15:17). Unless Christ took our sins as His own at His death, we will take them as our own sins to our death. Paul said, "Then those also who have fallen asleep in Christ have perished" (1 Corinthians 15:18). But Jesus did arise from the grave, and death for us has been "swallowed up in victory" (1 Corinthians 15:54).

The resurrection tells us that our sins were put into Jesus and He experienced the separation-condemnation for us. Thus Paul wrote, "There is therefore now no condemnation for those who are in Christ Jesus" (Romans 8:1). The grave can only hold the guilty. The only guilt Jesus had was ours. Because of our sins, He was separated from God; but when God forgave *our* sins, Jesus had no sins left of His own to condemn Him. Therefore, alienation was followed by a reunion. The Spirit of God filled the buried Jesus; the grave cannot hold the Spirit that created it. The grave became as a womb ready to give forth life. Peter explained it well: "God raised Him up again, putting an end to the agony (word for birth-pains) of death, since it was impossible for Him to be held in its power" (Acts 2:24). Paul declared that Jesus was raised by the Spirit of God in Him (Romans 8:11).

The bodily resurrection of Jesus is an historical fact that cannot successfully be discarded. All attempts to do so call for more belief in the incredible than that of the bodily resurrection of Jesus (see Gary Weedman's *Jesus,* Standard; and John Stott's *Basic Christianity,* Intervarsity Press). The Bible records at least nine bodily appearances of Jesus to people: Mary Magdalene (John 20:11-16); other women (Matthew 28:9); two on the road to Emmaus (Luke 24:13-31); Peter (Luke 24:34; 1 Corinthians 15:5); to ten apostles in the upper room (Luke 24:36-49; John 20:19-23); to the eleven apostles (John 20:26-29); to James, the Lord's brother (1 Corinthians 15:7); to the apostles by the sea (John 21:1-14); to the eleven by the Mount of Olives (Luke 24:50-53; Acts 1:6-9). After the ascension Stephen (Acts 7:55, 56), Paul (Acts 9:1-5), and John (Revelation 1:1-20) were permitted to see Him although not bodily. At one time, He appeared bodily to more than five hundred (1 Corinthians 15:6). We do not know how many other appearances He made like that. Perhaps thousands of people saw Him. There is empirical evidence for the resurrection, not just an existential feeling. He was seen with the eyes, not just with the mind; He was touched with the hands, not just with the heart (1 John 1:2; John 20:27; Luke 24:36-39). He listened, spoke, ate, taught, built a fire, and walked before witnesses.

Only a real resurrection can explain how Peter, who was afraid to admit to an insignificant maiden that he knew Jesus (John 18:17), could later refuse to keep silent about Jesus before the significant masters of men (Acts 4:19, 20). Only a real resurrection can explain why the early rumor that soldiers had stolen the body (Matthew 28:12-15) was never repeated by the opponents of Christianity. The real resurrection was not questioned by the Jews at Pentecost (Acts 2:24, 37), by the lame man (Acts 3:8), by those present in the temple area (Acts 3:15), by the council (Acts 4:1-22), by Paul (Acts 9:1-22), or by the Roman officials — Felix (Acts 24:15), Festus (Acts 25:13-19), or Agrippa (Acts 26). None of these people who were in a position to know reality questioned Christianity in its central teaching: "But God raised Him." Those who dealt with the philosophy of ideas (like the Gentiles) questioned it, but those who dealt with the evidence of history did not.

During Jesus' post-resurrection days on earth, He taught the apostles all that was written about Him in the Old Testament and opened their minds to understand these Scriptures (Luke 24:44, 45). He had previously assured them that His Spirit would guide them into all truth and cause them to remember everything He had said to them (John 14:26; 16:12, 13). And before His ascension, He breathed that Spirit upon them (John 20:22). Thus what the apostles said about Jesus and how they used the Old Testament are divinely inspired. To question what they said about Him is to question Jesus himself.

Now that the extended presence of God (the Holy Spirit) can again live in man since the barrier has been removed, Jesus' bodily presence is no longer needed. It would be better for all men that He go (John 16:7); for when He was on earth, His presence was limited to space and time. However, when He left and sent His Spirit, His presence is not limited; now He lives in many bodies.

Thus Jesus' ascension was necessary for the coming

of the Spirit. The apostles saw Him go (Luke 24:50, 51; Acts 1:9) and kept gazing into Heaven (Acts 1:10). But God wanted them soon to go everywhere declaring that Jesus was alive and the way to salvation (Matthew 28:19, 20; Luke 24:47). He is not interested that we keep our heads toward the sky, but that we look all around us and be used by God to restore the kingdom of God within the kingdoms of men.

Follow-up Questions

1. Discuss the meaning and relationship of ransom, redemption, reconciliation, righteousness.

2. Why did Jesus pray, "Let this cup pass"?

3. Why was Jesus' kind of life important to His kind of death?

4. What is the significance of "My God why hast thou forsaken Me"?

5. Discuss how Christ's death can become ours.

6. Discuss the significance of the resurrection.

12

The Kingdom Restored

Acts

The apostles knew that Jesus manifested the five characteristics of the kingdom: He was the Messiah, He forgave, He was righteousness in person, His life was filled with the Spirit, and He crossed all human barriers to demonstrate God's love for all people. The apostles rightly understood that all the Old Testament Scriptures referring to the coming king were fulfilled in Jesus (Luke 24:44, 45). So it was natural for them to ask about the restoration of the kingdom about which Isaiah had spoken (Isaiah 1:26; 49:6). But they asked about it with ethnically narrow attitudes, "Lord, is it at this time You are restoring the kingdom to Israel?" (Acts 1:6). The prejudices instilled within them from their Jewish traditional teaching did not yet allow them to include all peoples in the restoration. They did not understand what Jesus meant when He included "all nations" in His commission (Luke 24:47; Matthew 28:19).

Part of the reason for their narrow attitudes was their misunderstanding of who made up the "Israel" about which Isaiah spoke. They assumed it included only those who were identified as the offsprings (plural) of Abraham, but it included those who were to be identified with the offspring (singular) of Abraham who was Christ (Galatians 2:15, 16; 3:6-9; 3:29; Romans 2:25-29). It took the apostles more than a decade to accept this view. It is always difficult to rise above traditions — even for those who lived with Jesus in the flesh. And it is just as difficult for those today who live with Him in the Spirit.

As soon as the apostles asked that narrow question, Jesus replied with a universal answer, "But you shall receive power when the Holy Spirit has come upon you; and you shall be My witnesses both in Jerusalem, and in all Judea and Samaria, and even to the remotest part of the earth" (Acts 1:8). The book of Acts records the fulfillment of that promise; however, it is not a geographical expansion of Christianity as much as it is the ethnic expansion. If geography were Luke's primary interest, he would have told us what happened when many of the three thousand converts in Acts 2 scattered to all parts of the world, or where the Christians went as a result of their scattering in Acts 8:4, or what the Ethiopian eunuch did after Acts 8:29, or where Peter went after Acts 12:17, or where Barnabas and Mark went after Acts 15:39, or the activities of the other apostles.

Luke's primary interest was not in different territories reached, but in the different kinds of people evangelized and fellowshipped.

Luke was probably answering a question Theophilus (a Gentile) had asked (Luke 1:3; Acts 1:1). Perhaps he asked, "Who is correct? The Jews or the church? Who is really fulfilling the will of God? The Jews who want to keep me out unless I become a Jew first by circumcision, or the church which claims that God accepts me as a Gentile?" In the Gospel, Luke showed that Jesus was the promised Messiah who loved Gentiles as well as Jews. In Acts, he showed that the church did not pervert God's will but was performing it in accepting all kinds of people.

Embedded in the geography of Acts 1:8 are people distinctions: Jerusalem — Jews; Judea — people of the land; Samaria — half-breeds; ends of the earth — Gentiles. Although Christianity spread to the ends of the earth geographically immediately following Pentecost, it did not spread to the Gentiles for a decade (Acts 8:

26-39; 10; 11:19-21). When it did touch them, some internal problems were created (Acts 11:1-3; 15:1-29; 21:27-29; Galatians 2:11-14). Had there been no internal problems, Paul would not have had to write most of his epistles.

The restoration of the kingdom began in Acts 2. This event fulfilled both John's prophecy (Acts 1:4, 5) and Joel's (Acts 2:17-21). That Peter connected Joel's prophecy to the same event that Jesus had connected to John's prophecy makes it clear that the words of John, "He shall baptize you in the Holy Spirit," referred to an act that would identify the *beginning* of the new age or kingdom, for that is what Joel's prophecy signified. However, Joel's prophecy was not completely fulfilled on Pentecost, for he said, "I will pour forth of My Spirit upon *all* mankind" (2:17). We have already noted that "all mankind" meant Jews and Gentiles, not every person (see chapter 8). Only the Jews experienced this phenomenon at Pentecost (Acts 2:5, 6); therefore, the *beginning* of the new kingdom was *not finished* on Pentecost.

However, the kingdom had definitely *begun to begin,* for Peter made it clear that forgiveness and the Holy Spirit as an indwelling presence were available (Acts 2:38), and righteousness followed (Acts 2:42-47). Some human barriers were being crossed. The poor were being cared for (Acts 2:44, 45; 4:32; 6:1-6); the sick were ministered unto (Acts 3:1-10; 5:15, 16). Both men and women (Acts 5:14), common folk (6:1), and priests (6:7) were evangelized and fellowshipped.

Until Stephen's speech, only the Jewish rulers opposed the movement of Christianity. They did not oppose with physical force because they feared the population (Acts 4:21; 5:26). But Stephen (7:1-53) clearly announced that God's concern had never been restricted to only one "holy land," one "holy people," or one "holy temple." The idea was planted that Christianity would broaden beyond Judaism. This stirred opposition among the people. Saul saw the dangers involved and led in a persecution (8:3).

It took this persecution to move Christians to evangelize others besides Jews. Out of the scattering from that persecution, half-breeds (Samaritans) were evangelized (8:5-13), and an Ethiopian eunuch, on his way home from worshiping in Jerusalem, became a Christian (8:26-39). Although a Gentile, he posed no threat to Jewish Christianity because he was on his way out of the country and would not be present to fellowship with Jewish Christians. It was the fellowshipping, not just the evangelizing, of the Gentiles that threatened Jewish traditions.

Now that the conversion of Gentiles had begun, God would need a special man to teach the will of God regardless of the consequences to himself. God found that man in Saul. In Acts 9, Saul did not change his attitude about doing God's will — he had always done God's will as he understood it. But now he believed that Jesus was the Messiah. Saul was told to go to both Jews and Gentiles (Acts 9:15; 22:14, 15; 26:16-18). He would not permit anything to stand in his way of doing God's will. That was the kind of person he had been and the kind of man he would continue to be.

After the conversion of Paul (Saul's new name), God completed the *beginning* of His new age through Peter (Acts 10). It was not easy for Peter, with his Jewish background, to go into a house of a Gentile (10:28). In fact, he would not have fellowshipped with him had it not been for the vision and the command of God (10:11-16). Peter finally understood what Jesus meant in the Great Commission (10:34, 35). The Spirit phenomenon that happened on Pentecost happened again. The Jewish believers were amazed, but Peter knew that he must accept whom God had accepted; thus he baptized them (10:44-48).

Then the big test came; Cornelius asked Peter to remain in that Gentile home a few days (Acts 10:48). Will Peter fellowship with the ones of a different race whom he has evangelized? This is always the big test for the church also. We often get out of that tough decision by not evangelizing those with whom we will not fellowship. But Peter stayed; what followed is revealing.

The Jewish Christians criticized Peter—not for baptizing those Gentiles, but for eating with them (11:3). Cornelius, not the Ethiopian, presented a threat because he remained in the country. The Jewish Christians were aware of the responsibility of sharing with those evangelized. In essence, Peter said that he fellowshipped with them because God had made them his brothers (Acts 11:4-18). He made it clear that this was the fulfillment of John's prophecy (11:16). Since John's prophecy had already been connected with Joel's it would be completely fulfilled only when Joel's was. God's new kingdom had now *fully* begun. "All mankind" had been included.

Why did God take so long initiating the beginning? He knew the importance of continued fellowship to Christian growth. He knew that Jewish Christians would not have fellowshipped with Gentile Christians at an earlier time; they needed to mature. God's patience and love gave them time for it. It is only after more than a decade of maturation that we find the first integrated congregation in Christianity — Jews and Gentiles worshiping together (11:20). It was in that congregation that the disciples were first called Christians (11:26).

From this completed beginning of God's kingdom, Luke traced how Christianity crossed all kinds of barriers among people to become the religion for *all* people that God intended. It crossed political lines (Acts 13: 12), pagan religions (14:8-18), class differences (16:

14-34), philosophical lines (17:16-18), cultural lines, sects (19:1-7), superstitions (19:18, 19), emperor worship (19:31), and vocational lines. Anyone who believed in Jesus, repented, and was baptized was forgiven and became a dwelling place for God's Spirit (2:21; 2:38; 3:19; 8:12, 26-38; 9:17, 18; 10:47, 48; 11:21; 13:12; 16:14, 15; 16:25-33; 17:34; 18:8; 19:1-7).

As Jesus had demonstrated that God's kingdom was not shackled to any sex, class, political system, nation, or race, Luke showed that the church in Acts continued what Jesus began to say and to do. It was not easy. There was opposition from both within and without, but the church rose above it all to preach the kingdom of God and to teach about the Lord Jesus Christ "unhinderedly" (Acts 28:31). May this be the attitude of the church throughout the ages. May this be God's restoration movement!

Follow-up Questions

1. Does the opposition for crossing lines in evangelism and fellowship come mostly from outside the church or within it? Why?

2. What will be the basis for fellowship in Heaven?

3. Discuss John the Baptist's prophecy and Joel's in light of (a) their relationship to each other, and (b) their fulfillment in Acts.

4. Trace the ethnical expansion of Christianity in Acts.

5. Why did the Ethiopian eunuch pose no problem while Cornelius did? Relate that to present-day situations.

6. Openly admit the kinds of people against whom you hold prejudices. Why do you have them? Where did they begin? What is God's view? Relate 2 Corinthians 5:16 to this.

13

Kingdom Living

God's Family on Earth

The coming of God's new age did not erase the existence of the old age. Although God's sovereignty is universal, not everyone acknowledges that sovereignty. Only those who through faith have received the grace of God in Jesus Christ have been delivered from the evil age (Galatians 1:4). Christ has "delivered us from the domain of darkness, and transferred us to the kingdom of His beloved Son, in whom we have redemption, the forgiveness of sins" (Colossians 1:13, 14).

Christians have become partakers of the power of the new age — the Holy Spirit (Hebrews 6:4). It is that Spirit who has united us with God and with each other. This unity has created a family of God on earth (Ephesians 2:19) in which each regeneràted person is a member. It has created God's new Israel (Galatians 6: 16) of which each is a citizen (Galatians 3:26; Romans 2). We actually hold citizenship in two worlds — this world and Heaven. We must be citizens worthy of Christ (Philippians 1:27; 3:20; relate to the idea of the "Jerusalem above" in Galatians 4:26 and the "new Jerusalem" in Revelation 21:2).

How do we do that? God has called us to be His ambassadors (2 Corinthians 5:20); we must represent Him so that those who see us will give Him glory (Matthew 5:16; 1 Corinthians 6:19, 20; Colossians 1:27). The church is to demonstrate God's purpose to the watching world (Ephesians 3:9, 10). Since God's purpose is unity (Ephesians 1:9, 10), we must live lives of reconciliation with God and with other Christians. We must strive to reconcile those who are not Christians to God so that they too may enjoy the kind of fellowship they were created to enjoy (2 Corinthians 5:19, 20; 1 John 1:3).

A Life of Love

The mark of the reconciled life is love — *agape* style. *Agape*-love is the first fruit of the Spirit mentioned (Galatians 5:22). It is the product of abiding with Christ (John 15:9, 10). It is the characteristic of God that His children display (1 John 4:7). It binds everything together in perfect harmony (Colossians 3:14). Without this kind of love, all other activities are useless (1 Corinthians 13:1-3). It fulfills the requirements of the law (Romans 13:8-10; Matthew 22:37-40). It makes fellowship practical. Most of Paul's letters dealt with problems in fellowship, and it is probably still our basic difficulty in the church. The difficulty does not lie in lack of equipment but in a lack of maturity. Indiscriminate love is a mark of maturity (Matthew 5:43-48). It does not happen overnight. The Corinthians were spiritual babes (1 Corinthians 3:1) who needed to love. Paul's purpose was to preach and teach in order to present every man mature in Christ (Colossians 1:28, 29). The mark of maturity is love — "The goal of our instruction is love from a pure heart and a good conscience and a sincere faith" (1 Timothy 1:5).

Let us consider some practical expressions of love — *agape*-style. One is to continue to obey the commandments of God. Jesus said, "That the world may know that I love the Father, and as the Father gave Me commandment, even so I do" (John 14:31). And if we love Jesus, we will keep His commandments (John 14:15). John wrote, "This is love, that we walk according to His commandments. This is the commandment just as you have heard from the beginning, that you should walk in it" (2 John 6). Following God's commandments is not burdensome (1 John 5:3) if we are equipped with His Spirit (1 John 4:13). We do

106

not keep His commandments because we *have* to, as under the old covenant, but because we *want* to. Living God's way is now part of our new nature that is to grow up every way into Him (Ephesians 4:15). His commandments are commandments of love teaching us how to meet the needs of others. If we love, we will not steal because we care about another. If we love, we will not gossip because we care about another. "Love does no wrong to a neighbor; love therefore is the fulfilling of the law" (Romans 13:10).

Loving begins with proper attitudes about oneself. We are not to feel either inferior or superior (1 Corinthians 12:12-27). Although there are differences in function among us, we are not to consider ourselves better than others (Philippians 2:3). We are to associate with the lowly (Romans 12:16; James 2:1-9). We are to consider ourselves servants of our brothers and sisters in the family of God. Whatever charisma (gift) God has given to us is to be used for the good of others (1 Peter 4:10). We are to live to please others, not ourselves (Romans 15:1, 2).

We are not to create factions among Christians. Those who set up divisions by scoffing and murmuring are devoid of God's Spirit (Jude 16-19) and will destroy fellowship (Galatians 5:15). We are to lead the way in showing honor to others (Romans 12:10; 1 Corinthians 12:26). Each member should have the same kind of care for others without discrimination (1 Corinthians 12:25). We should contribute when others have material needs (Romans 12:13; Acts 4:32; Matthew 25:31-46; 2 Corinthians 8, 9; 1 John 3:17). Hospitality should characterize members of God's kingdom (Romans 12:13; 1 Timothy 3:2; Titus 1:8, 1 Peter 4:9; Hebrews 13:2). Is that characteristic fading from among us?

We are to live in a way not to injure the conscience of a brother (Romans 14:20, 21; 1 Corinthians 8). We are to treat weaker brothers with care (Romans 14:1). If a brother is overtaken with a sin, we are to help restore him, not condemn him (Galatians 6:1). We are to help one another carry burdens (Galatians 6:2). We must not use our tongues to hurt a brother but to help him (Ephesians 4:25). Bitterness, wrath, anger, clamor, and slander should give way to kindness and forgiveness (Ephesians 4:31, 32). All of the above expressions of the kingdom-life find their source in God's indwelling Spirit (Galatians 5:22, 23). If we have the Spirit, then let us walk by the Spirit.

A life of the autonomous individualist must give way to living within the community of unity. One man should not play "lord" over others. The greatest Christians are the ones with servant attitudes (Matthew 20: 20-28; Philippians 2:1-7). It is with the servant attitude of love that the unity of the Spirit is kept. Every Christian must give his energy to maintaining the unity of the Spirit (Ephesians 4:3). We are to strive for peace with all men (Colossians 3:15-17; James 3:17; 1 Corinthians 1:3; Romans 14:17, 19; 1 Corinthians 7:15; 2 Peter 3:14). Peace means absence of alienation (a useful exercise would be to search out and apply every usage in the New Testament).

However, God does not call us to have "peace at any cost." The only source of peace lies in the unity with Christ (John 14:27; Romans 5:1; Ephesians 2:14; Colossians 3:15). That unity is to be expressed not only in lack of alienation with God and others, but also in holy living (Colossians 3:1, 2). Without peace *and* holiness, no one will see God (Hebrews 12:14). The entirety of 1 Peter calls Christians to live holy lives amid an unholy environment. "As obedient children, do not be conformed to the former lusts which were yours in your ignorance, but like the Holy One who called you, be holy yourselves also in all your behavior" (1 Peter 1:14, 15). A life of holiness and a life of love are not opposed to one another. True love comes out of a holy heart (1 Peter 1:22; 1 Timothy 1:5; 1 Peter 4:8).

Peter's call "to abstain from fleshly lusts, which wage war against the soul" and to "keep your behavior excellent among the Gentiles" (1 Peter 2:11, 12) finds its application in: "Honor all men; love the brotherhood, fear God, honor the king" (1 Peter 2:17). Finally he said, "Let all be harmonious, sympathetic, brotherly, kindhearted, and humble in spirit; . . . for you were called for the very purpose that you might inherit a blessing" (1 Peter 3:8, 9).

God has called us into His family and wills that we live together now on earth as we will live together later in Heaven. And Christians do have a future. Kingdom life does not just involve the "now" generation. Jesus promised that because He lived we shall live. There will be a resurrection to an everlasting life with God (John 11:21-26; 1 Thessalonians 4:13-17; 1 Corinthians 15:20-22; 2 Corinthians 5:1). As God was faithful to His promise to old Israel, so His steadfast love remains faithful to His promises to us. We can be confident in our future as we trust His Word.

A Victorious Future

Earthly life may seem to threaten the fulfillment of God's promises that all things work for the good (Romans 8:28). Old Israel faced those threatening times. But she failed to remember God's promise, "I will bring you to the promised land." The people murmured and complained. Life will be just as tough for God's new Israel. But we have the advantage of knowing how God has always been faithful to His Word in the past. So through the maze of difficulties, the vision of John beams.

John wrote Revelation at a time when it looked as if all history stood opposed to the church having a victorious future. But God allowed John to see that through all the problems God was still on His throne (Revelation 4). While defeat looked evident at times, John saw a great multitude that no man could number from all ethnic groups around the throne (Revelation 7:9-12). He saw the community of unity free from its inhibitions. The balance of life was restored (Revelation 7:15-17; 21:1-4; relate to Romans 8:18). That great number he saw were those who had been regenerated by the death of Christ (Revelation 7:13, 14). These were the ones who would not disbelieve the promises of God amid the problems of men (1 Peter 1:3-5). They had remained faithful unto their first death (Revelation 2:7, 10, 17, 26; 3:5, 10, 12, 21). They had received the power of God that escapes the second death (Revelation 20:6, 11-15).

John saw that God's total family shall live together (Revelation 21:1-8) without the need for a temple of God (even our bodies as a temple; although we have new bodies), for He will be in our midst — not as an extended presence, but in all His reality (Revelation 21:22, 23). We shall see Him as He is (1 John 3:2) with the limitations of time and space gone.

He who is the Alpha and the Omega — the beginning and the goal of history — is coming and there will be judgment (Revelation 22:12). Those who have not accepted the death of Jesus as their own and the life of Jesus as theirs will be shut out (Revelation 22:14) to receive the wages their lives have voluntarily requested — eternal separation from God. With all its fullness they will experience Adam's separation from the tree of life (Revelation 22:19). However, all saved people will have an uninterrupted right to the tree of life (Revelation 22:14). Adam's past sin situation will have been reversed in all of its fullness. The gates will never be shut on the saved (Revelation 21:25).

But until He does come, life may be threatened. Satan is never idle (1 Peter 5:8). The world that re-